"Never in my life have I played harder than in Lancashire."

Sir Learie Constantine

'Rockets over Cribden'

The History of Rawtenstall Cricket Club 1886-2017

Celebrating 125 years of Lancashire League Cricket

First Edition

ISBN – 978-0-244-04131-1

© Roger Hindle 2018

Contents

Introduction

Acknowledgements

Page 7 - 12		The Early Days
Page 13 -24	1890 -1899	'The band played on'
Page 25 - 35	1900 -1909	'Take me out to the ball game'
Page 36 - 42	1910- 1919	'Till we meet again'
Page 43 - 51	1920 -1929	'Makin whoopee'
Page 52 - 59	1930 -1939	'In the mood'
Page 60 - 68	1940 -1949	'Rum and coca cola'
Page 69 - 78	1950 -1959	'Memories are made of this'
Page 79 - 85	1960 -1969	'Sunny afternoon'
Page 86 - 97	1970 -1979	'It's a kind of magic'
Page 98 -110	1980 -1989	'Just can't get enough'
Page 111 -121	1990 -1999	'Smells like teen spirit'
Page 122 -130	2000 -2009	'Beautiful day'
Page 131 -138	2010 -2017	'Price tag'
Page 139	Final thoughts	
Page 140 - 151	Appendices	Batting/ Bowling/ Wicket keeping records

The chapter titles refer to songs that were particular hits within the decade, whether they are appropriate or not…. you will have to decide.

Introduction

A man from Bacup writing a book about Rawtenstall Cricket – sacrilege! This was how news of my forthcoming publication was greeted by a few staunch Rawtenstall followers.

As a born and bred Bacup now residing in Rawtenstall, having been roped into Secretarial duties at the club by lifelong friend and legendary spinner Keith Roscoe and with celebrations taking place for 125 years of the Lancashire League, the time and occasion seemed about right.

My two previous books have focussed upon football in the Rossendale Valley. Having always been a fan of local cricket, my earliest memory is when my father walked me across Blackthorn Lane Bacup in 1970 to watch Australian professional Tony Mann and amateurs Roger Law and Barry Wilson, having a bat on the field at the tea interval and dreaming of scoring a century. I was hooked and attempted to play the game in my teens….without any real success. As with other failed cricketers I did what most of them did ….spent my time over the past 40 years watching, commenting, criticising and offering advice to many friends week in week out who played hard for their respective clubs.

The Lancashire League is known across the world and has witnessed the rise of many players to county and international fame. At Rawtenstall so many pioneers of the game have batted, bowled and fielded on the Worswick Memorial Ground. Famous names, legends and those with many a tale to tell. As you will find in the book, Rawtenstall have had their fair share of stars, characters and also-rans from both the professional and amateur ranks.

In today's modern throwaway society we recognise and value our buildings and monuments and list them for future generations. Let us also then acknowledge the sports fields that have been and continue to be a record of 125 years' worth of sporting heritage – they too need to be listed. At Rawtenstall who knows what the next 100 years will bring but hopefully it can provide an opportunity for some youngster out there dreaming to become the next Jimmy Anderson, Alex Hartley or maybe even Winston Place ,Peter Wood, Andrew Payne or Keith Roscoe.

The book incorporates a few social and economic historical events within the chapters, highlighting how Rawtenstall and Rossendale have fared over the past 125 years. I haven't forgotten the 'statos' though and there are a few tables at the back for the cricket aficionados. I am indebted to many people who have helped me put this book together and…. as a Bacupian I hope I have done Rawtenstall cricket justice!

Acknowledgements

Thanks to the following organisations, publications and individuals who have helped to make this book.

Bob Johnson

Crawshawbooth and District – Alderman Alfred Peel -1960

Lancashire Evening Telegraph

Lancashire League Website & Archive - Nigel Stockley

League Cricket in England – Roy Genders -1952

Peter Fisher

Peter Hindle

Rawtenstall Cricket Club

Rawtenstall Cricket Club - Centenary Souvenir Brochure - 1986

Rawtenstall Descriptive & Historical notes - 1966

Rawtenstall Library

Rossendale Free Press

Rossendale Reflections – William Waddington

Sandra Cole

See the Conquering Hero – David Edmundson - 1992

Steve Riley

The British Newspaper Archive

The Greatest Show on Earth – Noel Wild - 1992

The Early Days

A few newspaper clippings and the odd story passed down but more accurately including the informative words of Mr W.H. Hamer who captured most of the early information in his 1926 book charting the history of the club, indicate that the team we know today started in the Reedsholme area of Rawtenstall in 1867 although they had no club and pitch to play on; consequently all games were played away.

However newspaper reports mention a Rawtenstall team playing cricket in 1852. The earliest example of a game played is taken from the Blackburn Standard July 1852:

A match was played at Rawtenstall on Saturday last, between eleven of the Rawtenstall Club and the second eleven of the Blackburn Club. The gentlemen from Blackburn had the first innings, and scored 29 and 74. The Rawtenstall Club scored 35 and 32, and were consequently beaten by 30 runs. The day was fine, and the proceedings passed off to the satisfaction of all present.

The Manchester Courier reports of a game played between Bury and Rawtenstall at Bury on 13th July 1855. Bury scored 126 in one innings whilst the Rawtenstall men in two innings could only muster 17 and 65. A couple of months later they fared slightly better in the return fixture at Rawtenstall.

A copy of the Bury Times from September 1855 reports on the game.

Rawtenstall with Bradshaw, v. Bury with Six Men Barred. —This match, which had caused great interest and excitement in Rawtenstall and the neighbourhood, came off on the Rawtenstall ground, on Thursday last. The weather was all that a cricketer could desire, and consequently there was a large concourse of spectators, including a tolerable sprinkling of the fair sex. The Rawtenstall eleven having secured the services of their professional, Bradshaw, and also bringing into the field a very strong team, the result of the game was looked forward to with no small degree of anxiety by the friends of both parties. The match, however, in spite of these seeming advantages, we will venture to say, fell off from its predecessors in naught of interest or closeness. The state of the ground was beautiful, giving fine opportunity for the batsmen, and the scores would have been largely increased had not the same cause enabled the fieldsmen to combine boldness with safety, and activity with caution. The Rawtenstall eleven, having won the toss, sent in their opponents, eight of whom they contrived to shelve for 41 runs, when the gloom which had settled upon the hearts of the Bury eleven was speedily dispelled by the cry of "Collins to the rescue", and amidst the loud cheers of all present this true cricketer, ably assisted by Messrs. S. Woodcock and Beckwith, played one of his finest innings, and finally carried out his bat amid thunders of applause for a score of 14, leaving Rawtenstall to go in against. Mustering their forces on the field the Bury club were in doubt on whom to place the 'onus bowlandi'. The test of merit was, however, soon applied by short practice, and the result proved the efficacy of his mode of selection by calling upon Messrs Collins and W.P Woodcock to begin, by whose respective efforts, united with a well arranged field, their opponents was disposed of for 50. In their second innings the Bury marked 54, leaving Rawtenstall 67 to get a win. When the stumps were drawn at half-past five six wickets had fallen for 25 runs; therefore we have very little difficulty in seeing that the game was greatly in favour of the Bury club. After the game the rival elevens partook of a sumptuous repast, provided by the worthy host of the Queen's Arms, where, from the number of toasts that were given, we should say they had ample opportunity of proving the motto 'in vino veritas'.

The Rawtenstall team comprised of the following: T Chatburn, J Chatburn, J Townend, F Marchbank, J Parkinson, GE Hardman, T Ashworth, D Rawlinson, T Coupe, J Greenwood and professional Bradshaw.

A decade later the Rochdale Observer reports a game played in August 1856 against Rochdale and eight years later in July 1864 against Bacup:

On Thursday week, a match was played at Rawtenstall, between the second eleven of Rochdale, and the Rawtenstall club. In the two innings Rawtenstall scored 27, and 40, total; 67. Rochdale scored 47 and 33 total 74.

Cricket Match at Bacup.—On Saturday last, an exciting match was played at Lanehead between the 2nd eleven of Bacup and 1st eleven of Rawtenstall, resulting in a dead heat, each party scoring 112.

There is little else to find relating to this Rawtenstall team or the ground although we do find the Reedsholme club mentioned in 1867. The members of the Reedsholme team at that time included five Burton brothers, 2 Ashworths, 2 Pickups, 2 Sedgwicks, and men named Buckley, Hitchen, Duckworth, Holt, Lord, Sharples and Almond. All were asked to pay a shilling on the first Saturday in April and two pence a week afterwards. Players would have to walk miles for a game. Equipment was at a minimum and players participated without pads or gloves. On one occasion it is reported that a team ventured to Ramsbottom to play a side that sported top hats.

The Bury Times records a match by the Reedsholme club against Haslingden in June 1867:

Haslingden 2nd Eleven v. Reedsholme —a cricket match was played on Saturday last on the ground at Bentgate, between the above clubs. The play was good on both sides. The batting of R. Nuttall and J Poulton of the Haslingden team was excellent. The batting of F Whittaker, T Burton and E Ashworth of the Rawtenstall team was also good. The Haslingden club won with 19 runs to spare.

The Reedsholme team that day included the five Burton brothers.

Two years later a game took place again at Bentgate on 4th September 1869. This time it was against Haslingden first eleven. However they faced 22 players from Reedsholme and District! Haslingden scored 122 whilst the 22 players only managed 71 runs between them with R Ashworth (11) the only player to make double figures. The Reedsholme 22 included 3 Burtons, 2 Ashworths and 2 Whitakers.

Reedsholme also fielded a second eleven who played at Nimble Nook, an area of Chadderton near Oldham, in 1869 but could only manage to score 30 runs in reply to 122.

The industrial revolution was thriving and Rawtenstall would soon become a boom town in the Victorian era as families travelled from north, south, east and west to work in the mills and quarries established in the Rossendale Valley. From 1870 – 1890, over 3000 men were employed in the quarries that surrounded Rossendale. With the coming of the railway entire hillsides were quarried to build towns and cities all over Britain. There were between 15-20 mills in Rawtenstall alone - mainly cotton spinners and manufacturers but also bleachers and calico printers.

There is little else recorded regarding games played although by 1882 a ground was established in the Higher Constablee area of the town with the help from JE Haworth, a prominent manufacturer in the town who had a keen interest in the game. It was at this time that the club changed their name to Crawshawbooth. The Manchester Guardian covers a game between Colne and Crawshawbooth played at Colne on July 1882. Colne scored 82 whilst Crawshawbooth were 12 all out! There were now three Ashworths but only two Burtons playing for the club.

One of the first men engaged by the Crawshawbooth club was future Lancashire and England star Johnny Briggs (above and right). These early pioneers were employed to coach and teach locals how to play the game. Briggs (1862 –1902) was a left arm spin bowler who played for Lancashire

County Cricket Club between 1879 and 1900 and remains the second-highest wicket-taker in the county's history after Brian Statham. In the early days of Test cricket, Briggs was one of the most successful bowlers, proving deadly whenever wickets were affected by rain and was the first bowler in Test cricket to take 100 wickets. Briggs was a short man at about five feet five but his skill lay in his ability to vary the flight and pace of the ball as well as in achieving prodigious spin on the primitive pitches of the nineteenth century.

Briggs was not twenty years old when engaged by the Crawshawbooth club but paved the way to enable them to employ future professionals. The club employed Sam Holt of Todmorden as their first professional in 1883 for the handsome sum of £1 10 shillings per week (£100). The ground cost £9 per year rental (£600 today). Facilities were developed and a pavilion was purchased from Longholme Mill for the sum of £11 (£730) which was later transferred to the Bacup Road ground and used as a score box and refreshment room.

In 1884 George Nash was professional and by 1886 the club had relocated to the present ground on Bacup Road and changed the name to Rawtenstall.

Two Professionals played at that time - George Hardy and WH Wall. Wall was unavailable for the opening game so his substitute was Lancashire and England player R.G. Barlow (left). Barlow featured in a 24 run home defeat to Bacup and a 100 run defeat at Ramsbottom.

The Burnley Express covers the game between Burnley and Rawtenstall played at Bacup Road in late April 1886. Both Wall and Hardy played as did Johnny Briggs. Burnley were 147 all out with Briggs taking 5-46. Replying Rawtenstall were 98-8 with Briggs top scoring with 28 runs. The following month, Rawtenstall registered their first win in a friendly against Rochdale. Another victory came in July with a home win against Padiham – a young batsman by the name of Pickup was instrumental in the victory – more about him later.

Wall hailed from Bacup and was retained for the following season where he was joined by McIlvena who had also been professional for Heywood. To prepare the ground, a horse was sent from Constablee Bleach Works each week to mow the grass and at that time the wicket was set at a right angle to Bacup Road. In those days professionals were expected to perform a number of tasks, not unlike today, including preparing the pitch, repairing the ground, supervising practice, coaching players and of course win games for the club. In 1888 and the following year the club employed the services of 18 year old William 'Bill' Towler. A Yorkshireman from Yeadon, Towler would go on to play for the club as an amateur and key batsman making many runs from 1895 -1912. Off the field in 1888 the club paid £80 to have a pavilion erected on the ground which was officially opened on the 20th April 1889. The Athletic News reported on the home derby game against Haslingden on 10th June 1889. Below is a short extract

There are any number of "Derby Days" round about Bury, Ramsbottom, Accrington, Haslingden, and the Rossendale Valley, and I was at one on Saturday, when Haslingden and Rawtenstall met. My visits to football matches in the valley have been frequent, but Saturday was the first time I had seen a cricket match there. The experience of climbing up the mountains to find a football ground had caused me to go into training for the tour of discovering the Rawtenstall cricket enclosure, but I was surprised to find it in the only level spot Rawtenstall possesses at the bottom of the hill. And a very nice piece of turf it is and I was afterwards informed that a portion of it had been cut out of the hill, and that they intended to cart a few more hundred tons of ancient Rawtenstall away in order to make it larger. This will certainly be an improvement, for at present it is rather dangerous to sit and watch the proceedings with the probability of a big hitter giving you one in the eye. A pavilion has been erected during the winter months, and the one it has superseded comes in handy for a scoring box, but the club has been in existence but three years, and they intend having something better than the one they have recently built. They are well supported and Saturday being a glorious day there was a big crowd quite 3,000 and many of them came from Haslingden, which is situated on the other side of the mountains. The Rawtenstall band was in attendance, and played sweet music each time a batsman received his order. It was a well-conducted crowd too, and ladies evidently take an interest in cricket, for there were quite a number of them. There was only one outburst of loyalty, and that was when the Haslingden umpire would not allow Marshall to go out when he was stumped. They ought to do well, for very few clubs can raise 3,000 of a gate, and they are evidently well supported by the classes as well as the masses. The Haslingden professional Marshall, who has been doing very badly for his club, had some capital figures and was very hard to play. He sends down a medium-pace ball with a most peculiar delivery, which almost seems like a throw. This is what troubled the Rawtenstall men: **17.3 overs, 10 maidens, 15 runs, 7 wickets.**

The result...Rawtenstall were all out for 102 whilst Haslingden scored 205-6. It was early days and there would be plenty of time for revenge over the next 125 years. Rawtenstall Cricket Club was established...now for some proper competition.

The Lancashire League Championship Trophy

1890 -1899 The band played on

By 1890 cricket was established in most of Lancashire complemented by the energy and resurgence of many towns in East Lancashire. Cotton was King and for many areas it signalled their rise in status, wealth and prosperity. Populations increased as people came from all parts of the UK to work in the area. Rawtenstalls population grew significantly throughout the 1880's and 1890's reaching an all-time peak of over 31,000 people living in the town by 1891 as compared to 23,000 as it stands today. Within the Rossendale Valley the towns of Bacup, Haslingden and Rawtenstall quickly established their own civic identities and with that came rivalries and competition to be number one.

The Rawtenstall football club was also making news in the town having narrowly lost away to Ardwick (later Manchester City) in front of 2,500 spectators in the Christmas fixture of 1889. They also moved from their former ground above the cemetery to one opposite St James Church on Burnley Road in 1890 but disbanded in 1897.

Rawtenstall Cricket Club was keen to get the best possible players and advertised for a professional in The Athletic News on 15th July 1889:

WANTED First-class PROFESSIONAL for season 1890 for the Rawtenstall Cricket Club; a good fast bowler preferred.—Applications to be sent at once to JOSIAH BARLOW. Hon.Sec Rawtenstall.

It was TB Pullen with support from Nelson who were recruited as the paid men in the last season of friendly competitions in **1890**. The first game of the season was at home against Burnley on 12th April. The home game against Bacup in June brought a tight finish with Bacup scoring 113 with Hargreaves Hindle taking six wickets; however Rawtenstall fell just short and were 93 all out with Greenwood top scoring with 33. The following week though saw a victory over Royton with Pullen taking five wickets and scoring 27 runs.

In July the club engaged the services of Nottingham professional Wilfred Flowers (above) who scored 51 and took six wickets in the home win over Haslingden. In

13

September at home against Nelson it was Flowers and Pullen who again did the damage. Rawtenstall made 113 with Flowers hitting 63 and Pickup making 24. The other eight batsmen could only contribute a further 26 runs between them! Nelson were 85 all out with Pullen taking seven wickets. At the end of the season Read Cricket Club signed Rawtenstall amateur Hargreaves Hindle as their second professional for the 1891 season.

Below is the earliest known picture of Rawtenstall CC from 1890.

Back: J Stott (scorer) Hargreaves Hindle, Fred Pickup, T B Pullen (pro) JA Worswick, H Greenwood.

Seated: J Tomlinson, W Nelson (pro), J Meaken, H Burton, TH Heyworth, Jack Downes, Arthur H Taylor.

The major cricket event was taking place at the end of the season. On the 18th October a meeting was held at the Bull Hotel as recorded by the Preston Herald.:

Proposed Cricket League: On Saturday a meeting of cricket club secretaries was held at the Bull Hotel for the purpose of arranging fixtures for next season and other matters. Mr. J. Sutcliffe presided, and representatives were present from 24 clubs, chiefly in North-East Lancashire. Some discussion arose over the employment by some teams of six or seven professionals, which it was pointed out, placed some clubs at a disadvantage. The subject was deferred to a future meeting. The Chairman next introduced the subject of a proposed cricket league on similar lines to the football organisation. Mr. Hartley (Nelson) moved that a committee be selected to draw up a report showing the lines on which the league could be worked. This was agreed to and the following committee chosen Messrs. Lord (Bacup), Sutcliffe (Burnley), Hartley (Nelson), Whittaker (Accrington), Bradley (Church), Thompson (Whalley), Bentley (Ramsbottom), Wilkinson (Lowerhouse), Eastwood (East Lancashire), Nelson (Milnrow), Worswick (Rawtenstall), and Stephenson (Todmorden)

A week later on 25th October 1890 at the Commercial Hotel in Accrington the Lancashire Cricket League was formed. Rawtenstall were acknowledged as the youngest club to join the league – Colne Cricket Club cited as the oldest, with records going back to the 1830's.

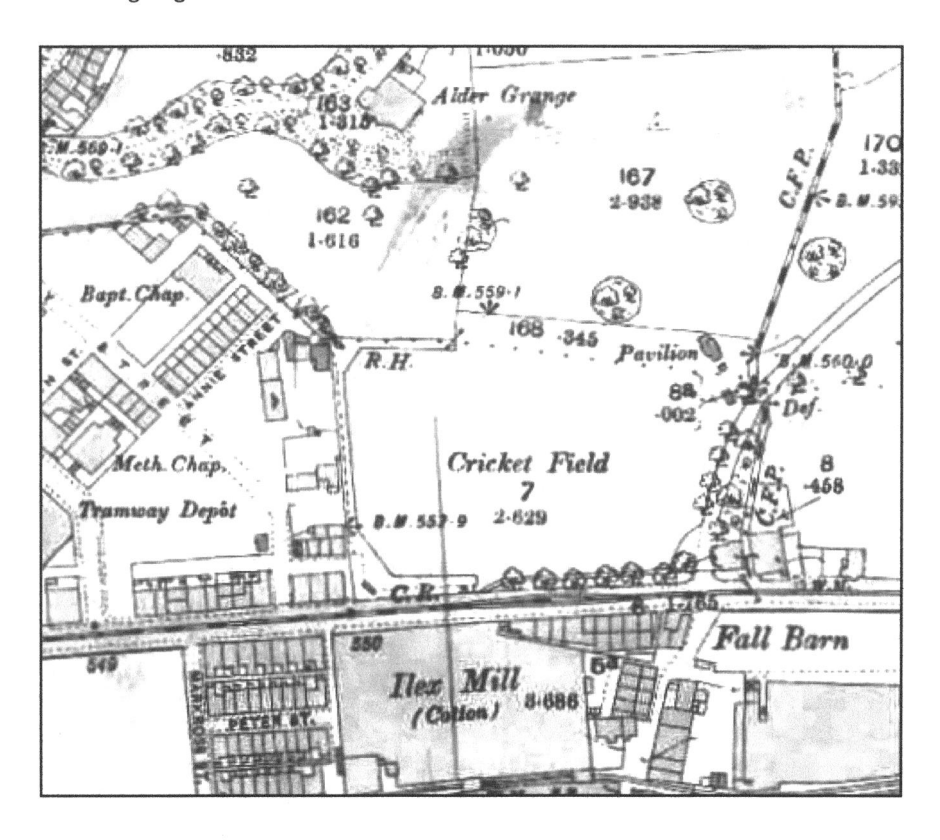

The Rawtenstall ground on Bacup Road from the Ordinance Survey map of 1890

The first season was **1891** and known as the North East Lancashire League and won by East Lancashire. For Rawtenstall it was a ruthless baptism and they finished next to bottom just above Accrington. Matches were very often low scoring affairs, none more so than the game at Lowerhouse on 12th September 1891. Rawtenstall were bowled out for 43 runs – Taylor (16) the only man in double figures. However Lowerhouse were skittled out for just 25 with Hindle taking 5 wickets and professional Bedford 4. Pullen and Bedford were the paid men that year each taking over 50 wickets apiece; amateur Hindle with 28 was the only other bowler in double figures. Pullen (248) and Pickup (239) were the leading batsmen.

When local teams like Haslingden visited gates of £17 were taken (worth approx. £1400 today) which would more than satisfy any club in the 21st Century. The two professionals would each take £1 (£85) as well as expenses from the gate fees.

There were other forms of entertainment and leisure taking place in the Rossendale Valley other than cricket and included brass band competitions with one taking place as recorded in the Burnley gazette in April 1891:

The Newhallhey Mills Brass Band held their first annual brass band contest and gala, on Saturday, in a field at Egypt Terrace, Rawtenstall. Twenty-one bands had entered, and 18 put in an appearance. £26 in cash was competed for as follows: First prize £12 (£1020), second £7, third £4, fourth £2, fifth £l.

The judge was Mr. J Shepherd, Liverpool, who gave his decision as follows 1, Goodshaw; 2, Heap Bridge 3, Change; 4, Haslingden Temperance; 5, Rawtenstall. A very large number visited the contest during the day.

Political Events

The first municipal election in the Borough of Rawtenstall also took place in June 1891. The borough was split into six wards each returning three councillors. The result was the election of 12 Liberals, 3 Conservatives and 3 Liberal Unionists. More political posturing was also taking place earlier in the year of **1892**, a by-election occurred to select the Member of Parliament for Rossendale. The election was held on 23rd January 1892 and was one of the most important political contests in the struggle over Irish Home Rule and a pointer to the outcome of the 1892 general election.

The Gladstonian Liberals selected John Henry Maden (right) as their representative. Maden was only 28 years old and was a cotton spinner and manufacturer, employing local people in Bacup. He was a Wesleyan by religion.

The weather played its part on Election Day. A heavy mist hung over the constituency all day but despite the poor weather it was estimated that around a 96% turnout had been achieved.

Maden was unwell in the last few days of the campaign and while he was briefly able to appear in public on the morning of polling day, he could not make it to the count at the Mechanics' Institute at Bacup where at about midnight on 25 January the Returning Officer, Colonel William Foster, High Sheriff of Lancashire, announced that Maden was the winner by a majority of 1,225 votes. Maden would continue to be MP for Rossendale until 1900.

1892 - The Lancashire League

Dropping the 'North East' from its title the following season **1892** the Lancashire League set out on its illustrious history with 13 teams (only Todmorden were missing). For Rawtenstall it would be a more promising season finishing in a mid-table equal 7th alongside neighbours Haslingden. Professional's Pullen (53 wkts +172 runs) and Albert Percy Charlesworth (46 wkts + 480 runs) performed well. A Yorkshireman, Charlesworth made seven appearances for the white rose men in 1894. Batsman Fred Pickup scored 569 runs including five 50+ scores. At the end of the season the league committee rejected an application from Padiham to join the league and also created a junior league for second eleven teams which was split into two divisions. Rawtenstall were joined by the three other valley teams plus Accrington, Bury and Church.

The big news in the town though was the disappearance of the town clerk for embezzlement of £200. The Lancaster Gazette reported the story:

THE DISAPPEARANCE OF THE TOWN CLERK OF RAWTENSTALL. Up to the present nothing has been heard of the missing Town Clerk of Rawtenstall (Mr. Walter Vere Stallon), against whom a warrant has been issued for embezzling £200.(£16,500). So far as the borough accounts are concerned, they appear to have been properly kept, and some of Stallon's friends clung to the hope that in the end all would be found right, even although he had written a letter confessing that he had misappropriated Corporation moneys. This hope was destroyed on Monday, when certain facts were brought to light which point to more than one serious offence having been committed. Mr. Procter, of Burnley, the borough auditor, who is examining the accounts, informed a correspondent on Monday evening that instances had been found in which persons had advanced considerable sums of money to Mr. Stallon on behalf of the Corporation, but which had never been handed over to the borough treasurer.

The full extent of the defalcations will not be known for another day or two. Mr. Stallon, it is stated, has for three of four years past acted as the trustee of an estate of about £3,000, (£250,000) which a young lady is entitled to when she attains her majority next month. Suspicion has been aroused that the funds of that estate may have been misappropriated, and that the dread of discovery and the consequences which would follow induced Stallon to abscond. His plans appear to have been well laid, for quite a week elapsed before any serious alarm was felt at his disappearance and inquiry instituted concerning him. Of course in that time he may have got well clear of the country.

Unfortunately there is no further reporting on the case of Mr Stallon – who knows where he ended up.

The cricket club was gaining momentum on and off the field and the following year finished fourth with Pickup again scoring over 500 runs for the season and Richard Green Hardstaff taking 92 wickets. The two professionals were Hardstaff and Thomas Nicholson – both well-built men who Rawtenstall would continue to employ in tandem for the next three seasons. Matches would often create disputes that required the League Committee to intervene and make decisions. They also requested that clubs should display posters around the grounds asking players and spectators to accept the decisions made by the umpires and remind spectators to behave. On many occasions fights and altercations between the fans would take place, more often due to drunkenness.

So as **1894** season started there was genuine optimism that this early success could be sustained. The annual general meeting held in January 1894 was reported in the Preston Herald:

The annual general meeting of the members the Rawtenstall Cricket Club was held in Co-operative Hall Tuesday evening, Mr. John Worswick in the chair. The statement of accounts showed that the adverse balance had been decreased from £492 to £487. The principal items of expenditure were professionals' wages. £143; (£12,000) stationery, etc., £25; rent; £30 interest, £19; cricket material, £25; match expenses, £14. The principal items among the receipts were: subscriptions. £122; gate money, £149; profit on garden party, £37; and profit on carnival, £13. The accounts were passed. It was stated arrangements were being made for a bazaar to be held in the spring, by which it is hoped to clear off the adverse balance. The following officers were elected: President. Captain Patrick; treasurer, Mr. J E. Haworth; secretary, Mr. R. Haworth; and a committee of twelve.

The bazaar in question took place over three days held at St Marys School. Incredibly this raised £962 – (worth approximately £58,000 today!) for the club it wiped out its debt and enabled it to focus on events on the field rather than off it. The Blackburn Standard reported on the outcome of the bazaar on 14th April 1894 and even then there was debate and opinion on the need for professionals.

Rawtenstall Cricket Club Bazaar. The Hon. William Brooks, J.P., of Crawshaw Hall, opened a three day bazaar on Thursday in St. Mary's Schoolroom, Rawtenstall, in aid of the funds of Rawtenstall Cricket Club. The stallholders comprise the leading ladies of the district, and the stalls are crowded with articles of a very valuable character. In opening the bazaar, the Hon. William Brooks said the object they were aiming at was to raise £1,000 to wipe out the debt upon the club. There was great satisfaction to him in the fact that the money had not been spent in paying men to play for Rawtenstall (Hear, hear.) He was quite sure that Rawtenstall men could play for themselves. He strongly protested against the system of professionalism, which was eating out all interest in their national games of cricket and football, especially football, and making them into a question of pounds, shillings, and pence.

Back on the cricket field - in one game Rawtenstall dismissed Haslingden at their Bent Gate home for just 21, Nicholson taking 6 wickets for just 4 runs! Nicholson was also prominent in the home win over Nelson, achieving a hat-trick where he cleaned bowled the last three Nelson men.

For the final Championship winning game of the season away at Church the team left in a coach, drawn by four grey horses followed by a convoy of wagons and supporters on foot displaying banners and flags. Church scored 107 all out with Nicholson taking 5 wickets. In reply Rawtenstall opener Arthur Taylor scored 75 to ensure the win and the clubs first Championship.

On the return to Rawtenstall crowds gathered and cheered at Accrington, Baxenden and Haslingden as the team paraded the cup with the support of Rawtenstall Borough and Goodshaw Bands. Refreshments were finally taken at the Queens Hotel.

The pavilion circa 1894 – the gentleman on the far right is Fred Pickup.

The season's statistics show that Hardstaff (98) and Nicholson (81) took all the wickets bar 17! Leading run scorer was the Captain - Fred Pickup (418). Pickup hailed from the village of Dean and served Rawtenstall well having been there at the very beginning in 1892 through to 1908. Other major contributions with the bat came from: George Hardy (350), Nicholson (314) and Arthur H Taylor (267). Gate receipts for the year came to £220 (approx. £14,000).

Back Row: Thomas Nicholson (pro) Fred Hamer, H Moore (scorer) Arthur H Taylor, Richard G Hardstaff (pro)

Seated: James Barrett, George Hardy, Fred Pickup (capt) Hargreaves Greenwood, Charley Womersley.

Front: Arthur Ashworth, James W Bush.

Rawtenstall League Champions 1894

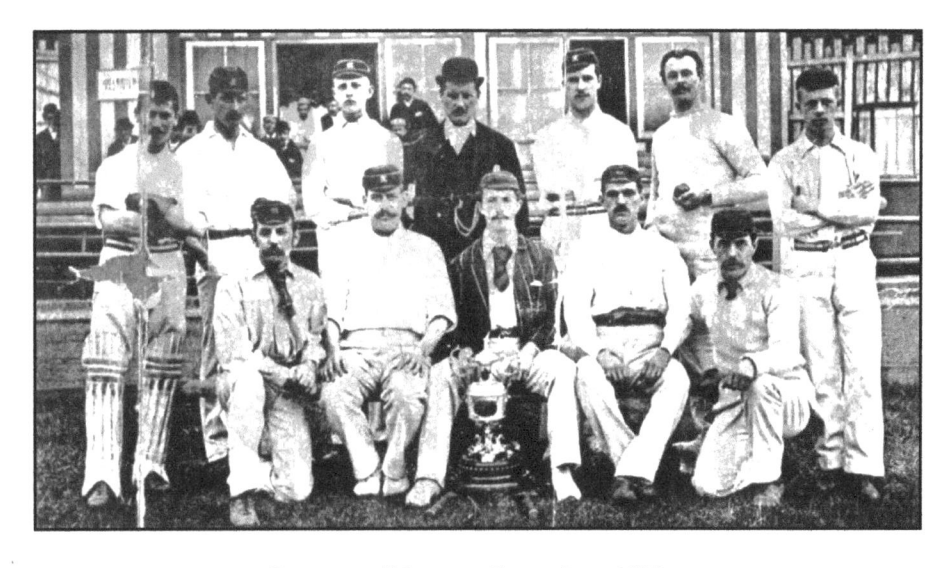

Rawtenstall League Champions 1894

Back: James W Bush, Thomas Nicholson (pro), Fred Hamer, H Moore (scorer) Arthur H Taylor, Richard G Hardstaff (pro), Arthur Ashworth.

Front: James Barrett, George Hardy, Fred Pickup, Hargreaves Greenwood, Charley Womersley.

The local paper, 'The Rossendale Echo,' issued a souvenir supplement which had the enclosed picture and profiles of each of the players. Particular highlights were noted about George Hardy who *"in 1893 took the Crown Inn of which he is still the jovial boniface"*.

Mad Dog at Rawtenstall

In November of 1894 it was reported that a large fox terrier dog was shot in the grounds of 'Brynbella,' Haslingden Road, Rawtenstall. A subsequent examination by a local vet showed that the animal was suffering from rabies. It was re-assuring to note that the last sentence in the report quoted that:

"The animal is supposed to have come from Haslingden or Accrington"!

Third place …. 3 times!

After the Championship win the next four seasons saw Rawtenstall maintain their excellent form finishing third on three occasions. On the 22nd June **1895** Arthur Taylor became the clubs first amateur league centurion scoring his one and only century (115) against Burnley at Bacup Road. Batting at no 5 he also passed 1000 Lancashire League runs in the same innings.

1895 also saw the first hat trick taken by an amateur bowler - Fred Hamer in the game at Enfield on 31st August, whilst in the same month Hardstaff took 9-33 in the home game against Colne. Again in August, Lowerhouse were dismissed for 34 with Hardstaff taking 6-17.

In the home game against Rishton in May, Nicholson took 6-9 to skittle the Rishton side out for just 31. George Hardy and Arthur Taylor both scored over 300 runs in a season and Hardstaff (90) and Nicholson (71) took all the wickets bar 31.

Hardstaff (pictured below) again was dominating the bowling statistics for the club in **1896** and was leading bowler in the league with 110 wickets for the season including 8-20 at Ramsbottom in May 1896. Nicholson took 63 wickets whilst Fred Pickup (453) and George Hardy (386) were the run scorers and an excellent third place in the league was attained behind Nelson and East Lancashire. In his four year stint as professional, Nicholson acquired 315 wickets.

The **1897** season saw good batting performances from the amateur men with George Hardy (531) including five 50's, Fred Pickup (488) and Will Towler (442) all scoring regularly. On the bowling front Hardstaff again was in good form with 81 wickets and he was well supported by Thomas William Foster who in 1894/95 had a season with Yorkshire. In his first season as professional alongside Hardstaff he took 62 wickets for the club. Burnley and Rishton were champions and runners up.

At home against Lowerhouse in April both Hardstaff (5-12) and Foster (5-13) were in fine form dismissing them for just 25. Hardstaff and Foster would team up as the paid men up to the turn of the century.

Foster had a particularly good season in **1898** taking 9-22 against Lowerhouse and 8-35 against Enfield in his total of 88 wickets which was equally matched by Hardstaff. Fred Pickup (506) again led from the front with the bat. This year it was Rishton and Nelson that took the top two spots.

There was more good news in the valley for residents of Bacup, Haslingden and Rawtenstall in October 1898 when the local sewage works opened at Ewood Bridge.

Flushed with the clubs success over the past three years, William Towler was the next to shine scoring a hundred and a big hundred it was. The year was **1899.** The game was against Haslingden at Bacup Road. Towler scored 156 not out and, similar to Taylor in 1895, also passed 1000 Lancashire League runs in the game. It was part of the highest team score in the league that year – 290-2 declared with George Hardy also scoring 69 not out. It was also a record third wicket partnership (182) for the club that stood for an amazing 116 years! A couple of weeks later Towler continued his grand form with another hundred (106) against Ramsbottom at Acre Bottom. 1899 also saw a third centurion for the club when Fred Pickup made the first of his four centuries in August against Rishton. Towler was the leading run scorer in the league with 695 runs. Pickup (452) and new boy Maden Chadwick Disley (363) were the other key contributors.

Disley could well be described as the first genuine amateur all-rounder the club had produced and the next two decades would see him make major match winning contributions.

In his eight years' service for the club Richard Hardstaff had taken 702 wickets. He was presented with a gold medal for his services. Hardstaff also took 100 wickets for his native Nottinghamshire 1887 -1899. In June 1896 he had his best all round performance for his County against Derbyshire where he scored 60 and took 8-53.

Richard Hardstaff bowling record for Rawtenstall

Year	Balls	M	R	W	BB	Ave	4wkt	SR	Econ
1892	122	6	62	6	4-25	10.33	0	20.33	3.04
1893	1861	120	731	94	**9-23**	8.12	8	20.67	2.35
1894	1820	112	746	100	7-18	**7.53**	13	**18.38**	2.45
1895	2042	107	885	90	9-33	9.83	9	22.68	2.60
1896	2480	**169**	894	**110**	8-20	8.12	**14**	22.54	**2.16**
1897	1814	99	865	81	7-12	11.68	8	24.51	2.86
1898	1794	97	786	88	8-35	8.93	10	20.38	2.62
1899	1806	101	833	67	8-46	12.43	6	26.95	2.76
1900	2016	73	929	66	6-17	14.07	4	30.54	2.76

The Lancashire League had quickly established itself although in the next century there would be further challenges. The first was from the League Committee who announced that from 1900 clubs would be limited to just one professional.

The other cricket ground in Rawtenstall in 1890 (below) was opposite St. James Church, on Burnley Road. Primarily used by junior cricket teams, including Longholme Wesleyan Cricket Club, it was also the home of Rawtenstall Football Club who played there from 1890 -1897. The ground was then sold for terraced housing which still exists.

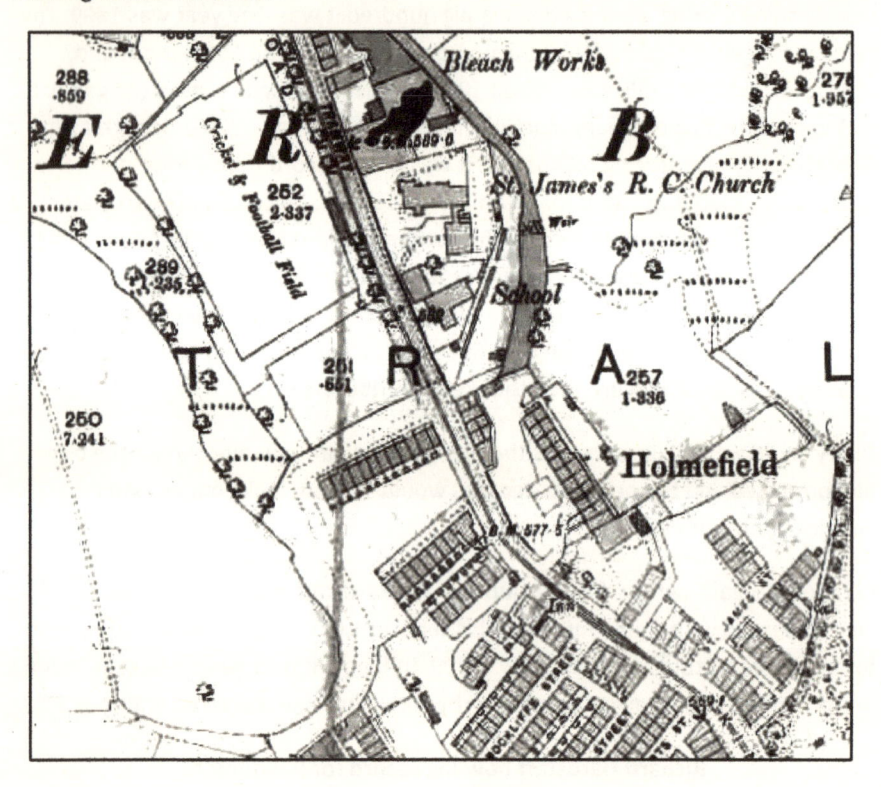

	P	W	D	L	Pts	Position
1891	19	5	5	9	15	12/13
1892	24	9	5	10	-1	7/13
1893	26	11	8	7	30	4/14
1894	**26**	**17**	**7**	**2**	**41**	**1/14**
1895	24	10	5	9	25	5/13
1896	24	12	4	8	28	3/13
1897	26	8	15	3	31	3/14
1898	26	10	10	6	30	3/14
1899	26	6	13	7	25	7/14

Best season of the decade in bold

1900 - 1909 Take me out to the ball game

Only four years since the inception of the Lancashire League and Rawtenstall faced a crisis! They would need to find a new ground as reported in the Lancashire Evening Post on 24th February 1900:

RAWTENSTALL CRICKET CLUB. A NEW GROUND REQUIRED. The annual meeting took place on Wednesday evening, Mr. J.A. Worswick presiding. The report and balance sheet showed the club had been less successful than in previous seasons. There were 109 less members, and an adverse balance of £28. The Chairman intimated that this coming season would be the club's last on the most conveniently situated ground in Bacup Road. The landowner had given them notice that he should require the land, and the club would have to look elsewhere for a ground. Land in the heart of the town was becoming very valuable, and was much sought after for building purposes. The rent of £30, (£2.350) received by the owner of the ground for its use as a cricket field, was only nominal compared with what would accrue from it as building land. The retiring committee have been looking out for an eligible site, but they've not yet one to recommend. Fortunately the club have a balance in hand of over £300. (£23,500)The balance sheet and report having been passed, thanks were heartily accorded to the retiring officials for their services to the club. The officials for the coming season were elected as follows: President, Councillor Peter Moore; Treasurer, Mr. J. E. Howarth; Secretary, Mr .R. Ashworth; Committee Messrs Fred Pickup, J.W. Stansfield, M. Handley, C.R. Hitchen. H. Greenwood. J. Stott, J. Halstead, T. Duckworth. J. Barrett. M. Mitchell and R. J. Taylor. Six of the retiring committee not re-elected. The new committee will face the ground difficulty at once, and seek to obtain a site. Sites of a suitable character are very rare in the district, and in the case of the most favourable ones, large expenditure would involve.

Thankfully for the club a rental agreement was reached with the landowner although a permanent solution would need to be considered.

The new decade started with each club allowed one professional and Rawtenstall continued with the services of the stalwart Hardstaff, who started his eighth continuous season with the club. He signed off with 66 wickets in an overall total of 702 in his 8 years and stands in second place in Rawtenstalls all-time wicket takers.

With just one professional the amateur bowling would have to respond and it certainly did in 1900 with Fred Hamer (44), Maden C Disley (34) and George Hardy (24) all contributing wickets. Pickup (622), Towler (406) and Disley (300) provided the runs which enabled fifth positon to be reached.

1901 saw the population of Rawtenstall reach its highest ever peak with just over 31,000 residents many of them working long hours in the many mills that adorned the town. The decade also saw a new industry start to thrive in the area and would continue to do so throughout the century. Over 3000 people were employed in the production of slippers in 13 factories.

In their limited free time the workers would now be able to enjoy the 28 acres of Whitaker Park (below circa 1901) which was purchased by Richard Whitaker and presented to the town. His desire was to "give the children of his native town a properly equipped and abundant playground". The park was opened by his wife on Saturday 3rd August.

The men's 'playground' at Bacup Road would see George Ramsbottom engaged for the year. Apparently it is said that he downed three pints before a game – as I am sure many others have done in more recent times...although perhaps after the match has finished. Maybe he was keen to prove his ability or maybe the beer was particularly effective at Liverpool Road Lowerhouse, as Ramsbottom took a career best of 9-15 on the first day of the season where 6 men were clean bowled. It's the second best bowling figures ever by a Rawtenstall bowler.

In all, Ramsbottom took 77 wickets for the season. Pickup was the leading scorer in the league with 767 runs including his second century, 130 not out against Nelson on 7th September. Disley (597) and Towler (476) also scored well.

Another impressive building was being constructed in the town. The foundation stone was being laid at one end of the ground. It would eventually become Kay Street Baptist Church and since then many a bowler has trundled in from that aforementioned named end.

Ramsbottom signed off to find beer elsewhere and in **1902** another man from Nottinghamshire was installed as professional.

Ben Taylor scored only 116 runs all season with a top score of just 19. Thankfully, he fared better with the ball in his hand taking 105 wickets and a best of 7-18. Staying just one year, he ventured on to Accrington for two years before going back to County cricket for his native Nottinghamshire. Rawtenstall finished fourth and the locals felt that a title wasn't that far away.

It didn't happen in **1903** although further recreation and leisure opportunities were being created in the bustling town. Plans for a new library, which would include a £6000 donation, worth today somewhere in the region of £470,000, from the philanthropist Andrew Carnegie were drawn up. A year earlier a letter from Carnegie was read out at a meeting of Rawtenstall Borough Council offering £6000 towards the building of a new library. The Public Libraries Act 1892-1901 was adopted in Rawtenstall on 28 August 1902 and this made it possible to accept the offer.

On the cricket field the year proved a thorough disappointment. There would be no title bid as Rawtenstall found the wooden spoon hanging from the dressing room wall with just one victory all season. Despite that there were some excellent personal performances. Two amateurs scored over 500 runs (Disley and Towler). Disley even scored two centuries at Todmorden and Haslingden so the batting talent was there. Professional Thomas Owen Thomas – no he wasn't from Wales, born just over the border in Hereford - took 67 wickets.

What Rawtenstall needed was a strike bowler or someone who would get teams out.

Well, Yorkshireman Thomas Stringer wasn't exactly a strike bowler in a modern day sense – he bowled leg breaks, however in **1904** he bowled Rawtenstall to their second Championship title. Maden Disley was the highest run scorer in the league that season even though he failed to register a century. Disley was a fine left handed batsman and also a useful left arm medium pace bowler. When not playing cricket he was treasurer for Rawtenstall Borough Council. Not far behind was Will Towler (670 runs) who was the club's professional back in 1888 and 1889 at just 18 years of age.

But it was the bowling of Thomas Stringer that won Rawtenstall the league. His figures are quite amazing. In the 26 games played he took 5 wickets or more in 18 of them, in fact he averages over 5 wickets per game. Stringer's leg breaks bamboozled the opposition batsmen. The man from Huddersfield, who played just one County game for Worcestershire in 1909, was exactly what Rawtenstall needed. With bowling support from Kelly (34) and Disley (33) and the batting of Disley (807), Towler (675) and Pickup (295). Rawtenstall had the amateur support to back Stringer. The penultimate game of the season was at home to Colne and victory would see the Championship coming to Bacup Road. Pickup wouldn't complete the season though as, in mid-August; he sailed to Canada with his father in law Mr Richard Whitaker on business. The local paper reported on the game against Colne:

At 6 on Saturday evening there was a scene of great enthusiasm on the Rawtenstall cricket ground, for at that time the last Colne wicket had fallen, and with it came victory for Rawtenstall, which made them champions of the Lancashire League. The home club batted first, and scored 162 for eight wickets, declaring at 4-45. To this Colne replied with 67 Stringer and Kelly each taking five wickets. Towler was the hero of the afternoon, amassing 85 in grand style, and as a reward the sum of £7 10s, (worth £450 today) was collected for him. Rawtenstall gate receipts this season are already a record, nearly £400 (£24,000) having been taken. The enthusiasm of the spectators knew no bounds. Hats and sticks were sent into the air, and some the players were literally carried to the pavilion. Here a great cheering crowd collected, and much amusement was caused when a number of young men appeared with a tin cup, and made a mock presentation to W. Towler, the officiating captain, who, amidst roars of laughter, received the trophy with smiling features.

Back Row: Jack Downes, Jim Jeffrey, Maden C Disley, Tom Stringer (pro), Tom Waller, Harold Hoyle, George Ashworth.

Seated: George Heys, Will Towler, Fred Pickup (capt), Joe Sunderland.

Despite winning the league six defeats would occur during the year and a rather heavy defeat at Bacup Road took place on 18th June. Burnley scored 227 - 9 declared. Rawtenstall replying were 25 all out - Jack Downes top scorer with 5 runs! The final game of the season was at Burnley on 10th September where the cup would be presented. The game itself was won by Burnley again but that didn't deter the celebrations that took place afterwards. The Rossendale Free Press gave a full account of how proceedings for the day would take place:

"The whole borough is anxious and enthusiastic about doing honour to the team"

11:30 am: Team will leave Queens Arms Hotel in a coach and four horses, with postilions and horn blowers.

12:15: Guarantors and committee will leave the Queens Hotel in a char-a banc and four.

12:15: Second team will leave in a wagonette.

12:30: Coaches and wagonettes will leave various hotels and clubs in the town.

1:30pm: Match commences at Turf Moor.

6:30pm (at latest) Match finishes, At the finish of the match the League Cup will be presented to Mr W Towler, the captain of the team, by Dr Crawshaw of Ramsbottom, the chairman of the League Committee. The cup will be brought by the League authorities from Nelson and will be on view at the ground.

6:30pm: The team and governing body will be entertained to tea at Crankshaw's Hotel.

7:30pm: Cavalcade leaves Burnley. This will be met on the homeward journey at the entrance to the borough (whether at Loveclough or Water is undecided) by Goodshaw Prize Band and about 300 torch bearers, with lighted torches. The procession will call at the house of the captain, Red Lion Cloughfold and finish at the Queens Arms Hotel. The band will then play a selection of music on the Queens meadow.

The route taken was via Loveclough where thousands lined the 6 mile route back to the town. It must have been quite a sight to see the lighted torch procession make its way to Rawtenstall.

More positive news came from the gate receipts for 1904 which came to an impressive £390 (£25,000).

Matches	Innings	N/O	Runs	Highest	Ave	100	50	Catches
25	25	2	807	94	35.08	0	7	14

Maden C Disley batting record for Rawtenstall 1904

Balls	Maidens	Runs	Wkts	Best	Ave	5 Wkts	S/R	Econ
2275	73	1084	133	9-32	8.15	18	17.10	2.85

Thomas Stringer bowling record for Rawtenstall 1904

Rawtenstall League Champions 1904

Back Row: Tom Stringer (pro) Mr Cronshaw (scorer) Tom Waller, Maden C Disley, Chris Sedgwick, Jesse Robinson (club secretary) Jack Kelly.

Middle Row: Jim Jeffrey, Will Towler, Fred Pickup (capt) Joe Sunderland, Jack Downes.

Front Row: Harold Hoyle, (wicketkeeper) George Ashworth.

Stringer was quite rightly engaged for **1905** but there was a reliance on Towler and Disley scoring the runs and whilst both men had good seasons with the bat Disley 479 and Towler 512, there was little support elsewhere. Towler scored another century, 128 not out at home to Rishton. On the bowling front Stringer (81) and Disley (33) were the top men.

The season proved a unique one insofar as all the valley sides finished in the bottom four places. One could say that Rawtenstall won the bragging rights in the valley as they finished the top side... albeit in 11th place.

Long serving batsman and captain Fred Pickup announced in April 1906 that due to ill health he did not foresee playing again. He had had several serious illnesses over 12 months and hadn't played throughout 1905. It was a severe blow to the club although Pickup had given excellent service over 14 years.

Back Row: J Stott, SF Stansfield, JT Lord, Robert Worswick, John A Worswick, M Handley.

2nd Row: T Duckworth, P Moore, C Sedgwick, JR Cronshaw (scorer) MC Disley T Stringer (pro) J Kelley, R Hitchen, J Robinson, JW Stansfield, H Greenwood, JA Lord.

Seated: R Waller, J Jeffrey, W Towler, F Pickup, J Sunderland, J Downes, C Sedgwick, and Front: H Hoyle, G Ashworth.

Rawtenstall League Champions 1904

The year started with the grand opening of the market hall and shops which had been constructed the previous year. The event took place on January 18th **1906**.

Saturdays and Thursdays were the designated days as they still are today.

Batting was not a particular quality that was forthcoming from the professionals Rawtenstall employed during the 1900's, none more so than this particular year when William Peach was engaged.

The Lincolnshire born man, who played just one first class game for Derbyshire, only managed to score 80 runs in the 16 innings at an average of just over 5. Amateur Disley showed how it should be done scoring 501 runs. His consistency with the bat provided an invitation to play in two second eleven games for Lancashire in the Minor Counties Championship, opening the batting against Yorkshire (34 & 9) and Surrey (0 & 14).

Peach took 47 wickets and Bob Waller 43 wickets for the season.

Prior to the start of the season the club accounts were not in the healthiest of states as noted in the Manchester Courier on 24th January 1907:

RAWTENSTALL CLUBS HEAVY LOSS. The balance sheet of the Rawtenstall Cricket Club, just issued, shows loss on the season's working of £101 6s. 6d., (£8000) accounted for by the heavy expenditure in repairing and painting the whole of the woodwork and ironwork on the ground, the relaying of a large portion of the ground, the bad weather in three or more attractive home fixtures; and the moderate position the club held in the League table. The largest gate was the match v. Haslingden, when £32 3s. 7d. (£2,525) was received. M. C. Disley won the batting and R. Waller the bowling prize.

On the playing side **1907** proved slightly better with George Ramsbottom being re-signed as professional for the next three seasons after first playing for the club in 1901 – perhaps he liked the beer at Bacup Road which was provided by The Crown pub just down the road (who sold it to the club). A beer tent was regularly set up at the Kay Street end and, according to old reports; there were frequent 'airings of opinions' and 'fisticuffs'.

The facilities in the town were really shaping up and the new impressive library was opened in 1907. The Carnegie inspired building engaged Hargreaves Wilkinson as the first librarian who clearly enjoyed his job as he stayed there for 32 years!

The library, to this day, is one of the finest buildings in the town and a stunning example of architecture and craftsmanship well worth a visit and rightly given Grade II listed status.

The new Carnegie library opened on 1st June 1907.

Rawtenstall Library with Hargreaves Wilkinson (centre).

On the field the Lowerhouse players were struggling to read Rawtenstall professional Ramsbottom's bowling as he took 7-17 including five clean bowled. Ramsbottom amassed 73 wickets well supported by Bob Waller (55). The runs came from Will Towler (474) including 90 not out in the last home game against Accrington in a season that ended in mid-table. Further success though came with the news that the second eleven had secured their first Championship triumph.

Ramsbottom was amongst the wickets again in **1908** with 94 scalps backed up by the amateurs Waller (48) and George Ashworth (35) in fact the three bowlers took all the wickets bar 13! Pickup returned after ill health to play just another six games before finally calling it a day. A young 17 year old was making his debut that year and took one of the 13 wickets and scored 161 runs in the 15 matches he played, nothing spectacular there you may say but there would be more to come from this talented young man over the next two decades... his name?... Alfred William Pewtress. It was another batsman that grabbed the headlines though – Maden Disley notched another 552 runs including his highest ever score -150 not out against East Lancashire.

Fred Pickup's jacket and cap currently displayed in the clubhouse.

34

Year	Matches	Innings	NO	Runs	Highest	Ave	100	50
1892	20	20	2	569	79	31.61	0	5
1893	23	23	1	548	62	24.90	0	4
1894	24	23	4	418	65*	22.00	0	2
1895	22	22	2	274	53*	13.70	0	1
1896	21	20	0	453	72	22.65	0	1
1897	21	21	1	488	66	24.40	0	4
1898	20	20	1	506	87	26.63	0	4
1899	16	16	1	452	104*	30.13	1	3
1900	22	22	4	622	108	34.55	1	4
1901	**21**	**21**	**4**	**767**	**130***	**45.11**	**2**	**5**
1902	20	20	1	503	62	26.47	0	3
1903	13	12	0	124	46	10.33	0	0
1904	16	16	1	295	87	19.66	0	2
1908	6	6	0	177	52	29.50	0	1

Fred Pickup's batting record for Rawtenstall

The **1909** season proved difficult with the bat as no-one scored over 350 runs. Top scorer was Fred Haworth with 303. Bowling wise Ramsbottom, in his final season, took 60 wickets including 8-16 at Lowerhouse but with only four victories all season it was a disappointing end to the decade.

Off the field, at the top of the bank behind the ground, Alder Grange School was being constructed. Tenders had been invited in June 1908 and construction took place in 1909. The school would accommodate about 650 pupils and the cost, including furnishing, would be £9350 (£730,000). In January 1910 Headmaster Mr John Watson had been appointed, former head of Water County School.

	P	W	D	L	Pts	Position
1900	26	8	11	7	27	5/14
1901	26	9	7	10	25	8/14
1902	26	12	6	8	30	4/14
1903	26	1	13	12	15	14/14
1904	**26**	**15**	**5**	**6**	**35**	**1/14**
*1905	26	5	13	8	23	11/14
1906	26	6	11	9	23	10/14
1907	26	9	9	8	27	7/14
1908	26	6	7	13	19	11/14
1909	26	4	10	12	18	13/14

Best season of the decade in bold

* All valley sides finished in the bottom four places

1910 - 1919 Till we meet again

An Australian, a Yorkshireman and a Maltese man …No, not some bad taste joke but men who would feature in Rawtenstall colours during the decade.

It would prove a difficult one for Rawtenstall in many ways as the town, like many in East Lancashire, would feel the full force of war and everything that such atrocities bring. Many young men from the town would join up similar to their Accrington Pals down the road, making as they did the supreme sacrifice.

On the hill above the field Alder Grange school had opened to replace Longholme Wesleyan School at a cost of £11,000 to accommodate infant and mixed classes. The school later became a Secondary Modern. One wonders how many scholars of the game of cricket the school has produced over the years who have represented the club.

The year started well for the town with news that The Bleachers' Association had bought both Cloughfold and Constablee Bleachworks which had been closed for over 12 months. When the works were restarted it gave employment to over 100 operatives from the town.

On the cricket front Rawtenstall rarely finished in the top half of the table, the only two exceptions being 1914 and 1919. However strong individual performances were to be seen throughout.

Now the name - John Elicius Benedict Bernard Placid Quirk Carrington Dwyer (above) may not be one that rolls off the tongue that easily for many but for Rawtenstall it would be their first venture into employing an overseas professional. The man from Sydney, Australia had been employed by Sussex County Cricket Club from 1904-1909 and had scored 986 runs and taken 179 wickets for them in 61 first class matches.

Engaged for the **1910** season at Rawtenstall he would struggle with the bat scoring just 182 runs, 92 of which occurred at Todmorden. However he performed better with the ball taking 83 wickets including 7-43 away at Church and 7-48 at home, against Enfield.

It was amateur Disley who produced the runs and he was scoring freely. In three consecutive games he scored 95,102 and 92, again reaching over 500 runs for the season. George Ashworth (305) was the other significant contributor. Dwyer was supported with the ball by Jack Kelly who took 60 wickets including 7-34 at home to Colne. There was though some success for the club and Dwyer. The Rossendale Cup was established and competed for by the 4 valley sides for the first time in 1910. The Lancashire Evening Post reported on this new competition:

ROSSENDALE VALLEY CUP Competition. At a meeting of representatives of the Bacup, Rawtenstall, Haslingden, and Ramsbottom cricket clubs, held at Rawtenstall, it was resolved to promote a new cricket competition, to be known as the Rossendale Valley Cricket Championship Cup Competition. The four League clubs named will be the competitors, and the winner of the final tie will be presented with a silver cup, to hold for a period of twelve months. The matches will commence at the customary hour, but will be played to a finish, or, if necessary, for as long as the, umpires shall deem the light sufficiently good. The draw for the semi-final tie has been made as follows: Bacup v. Ramsbottom, Monday, August 8th Rawtenstall v. Haslingden, Monday, August 22nd. The matches to take place on the grounds of the first named. The gates are pooled, and each club will play a league team and the professional.

Rawtenstall won the semi – final game and would face Ramsbottom in the final. Played at Bacup Road the match attracted an impartial crowd drawn from all parts of Rossendale. The gate receipts were £41 (£3,200). Rawtenstall were bowled out for 133 - Pewtress top scoring with 44. However Ramsbottom were skittled out for just 89 with Dwyer and Waller each taking 5 wickets. The cup would be re-named The Maden Cup in subsequent years.

Only employed for one season the sad postscript to Dwyer's story is his early and untimely death just two years later, in Crewe, at the age of just 36.

This decade though would also see the rise of a young batsman who would go on to provide Rawtenstall and Lancashire with dedicated and loyal service – in the case of Rawtenstall over 20 years. Having made his debut in 1909 as a 17 year old Alfred William Pewtress or 'Fred' as he was known to most, would soon be leading by example.

On the leisure front the town had the aptly named Grand Theatre to entertain the population. It was granted a Cinematograph Licence in 1910, and became a full time cinema. During World War I it went back to live theatre use and was re-named Palace Theatre in 1918. It was not a successful theatre, and even a name change to Palace Theatre of Varieties did not help increase business.

The **1911** season saw some excellent performances with the bat. Robert Waller led the way with 544 runs. 'The old pretender' - forty five year old Will Towler was still racking them up with 463, whilst 'the new kid on the block' - Pewtress (left) was not far behind with 459. Professional Harold Harrison, a Yorkshireman with two first class games for the County, contributed 477 including a hundred at Haslingden and 68 wickets, but too many drawn games ensured a mid – table position would be attained. Waller (30) and Kelly (28) were also amongst the wickets. The home defeat to Todmorden in August required the umpire – Stephenson of Nelson- to be safely escorted off the ground by police. The local crowd had gathered around the pavilion at the end of the game and *"showed their disapprobation by hooting"*.

The **1912** season saw no-one really grasping the nettle with the bat except Towler - again scoring his customary 462 for the season was the only one on real form. Harrison took 81 wickets with his left arm spin including 8-20 at home against Rishton. James Stansfield (33) led the amateur bowling. The drawn games were reduced but another mid –table finish would be obtained.

As the **1913** season was approaching more disturbing events were taking place nationally and internationally. However cricket would carry on for the time being and Rawtenstall employed George Leach (1881 -1945) as professional for the next three years. The 32 year old Leach, who was born on the island of Malta, stood at 6ft 4" and, similar to John Dwyer, had been employed by Sussex County Cricket Club for the past 10 years. A fast bowler and right hand bat he frightened the wits out of many players just running up! The most noted of occasion being the 28th June 1913. Leach stormed in taking 9-32 at Enfield all of which were bowled! A total of 102 wickets and 398 runs, including a hundred at Church, convinced the Rawtenstall committee to employ him for a further two seasons. Fred Haworth with 62 wickets was excellent support to Leach (right). His best figures were 7-34 at home against Enfield including five clean bowled. Pewtress, who was now captaining the side at the age of 22, led with the bat scoring 558 runs. He was well supported by Harold Clegg (433) but losing half the games meant another disappointing season.

There would be something to cheer at this difficult time, as celebrations were taking place in town with the visit of King George V and Queen Mary. Staging was set up opposite the town hall to cater for the Royals and help the thousands gathered to catch a glimpse. Local schools were balloted to determine where they would stand. All the factories closed at noon and every vantage point was taken.

The King and Queen were welcomed by the Mayor and Mayoress, Councillor Joseph Grimshaw and Miss Smith. The year also saw the opening of Bacup and Rawtenstall Grammar School and, like the Royal family it is another institution that has lasted well. The school was acknowledged as one of the best in the county and continues to be so in the 21st Century, and over the years has provided many cricket scholars for the club.

The year **1914** is etched in the minds of many as the beginning of The Great War which would dominate the lives of many for the next four years but first there was some cricket to warm the hearts of the Rawtenstall faithful and indeed it did with what would be their best performance throughout the decade.

There was some good news to start the year as in April it was announced that eight alms-houses would be built opposite Whitaker Park from the £10,000 legacy (£590,000) from benefactor Richard Whitaker. The figure also included two scholarships for Rawtenstall youngsters. The houses still stand to this day.

Back to cricket and Alfred Pewtress (right) was in magnificent form hitting two centuries – firstly 101 at home to East Lancashire on 30th May followed by 122 not out against Rishton at home on 11th July. Earlier in May Pewtress was invited to play for Lancashire second eleven against Cheshire.

The Manchester Evening News reported that:

Pewtress, who is only about 23 years of age, is a clever young batsman, and so far this season has shown capital form, having scored 168 runs in four completed innings. Last season he headed the club averages, scoring 558 runs in 22 innings, his average per innings being 25:36. The selection has caused great satisfaction in Rawtenstall, where Pewtress is very popular.

His 838 runs for the season were the highest in the league, as was his average of 44.26. With two 100's and five 50's it was no wonder that he was attracting the interests of Lancashire. He was supported by professional Leach, who hit a century on the opening day of the season followed by two 50's, in a total of 548 runs and Harold Clegg (465). Leach again with the ball (80) and George Ashworth (47) enabled Rawtenstall to have their best season in the decade and finish in equal fourth position with Church. Success also came in the Maden Cup – this time Haslingden (the holders) were the visitors to Bacup Road. The rules were each side was allowed two hours batting – the team scoring the largest number of runs be declared winners.

Pewtress won the toss and elected to bat. Leach scored 73 in Rawtenstalls total of 162. Haslingden failed to make three figures and the cup was presented to Rawtenstall by Alderman J H Maden JP.

The Waller Brothers -Tom and Robert - were the mainstay amateur batsmen for the **1915** season. An opening partnership of 191 between Leach and Tom Waller at Ramsbottom was one of the highlights of the season and a record that stood for 69 years. The other highlight came from Leach again who took 9-55 at East Lancashire in July – the other wicket was taken by Fred Haworth albeit caught by Leach! The professional led the way with 680 runs (including two centuries) – the first professional in the club's history to achieve this feat in one season. The Wallers - Tom (396) and Robert (355) offered valuable support. On the bowling front Leach (82) and George Ashworth (39) performed well in a season where several of the players joined up to support their country in The Great War. Leach clearly enjoyed his life in the valley. He was employed at the local gas works and later married a local woman – the landlady of The Sun Inn. He continued to live in Rawtenstall and died aged 63 in 1945.

Between **1916 and 1918** there were no professionals employed by clubs as teams would endeavour to field a full side to compete. The first game of the 1916 season saw James Stansfield take 8-40 to bowl Church out for 157 however Rawtenstall were then bowled out for just 33. Another player, Fred Haworth, also took 9-21 at home against Burnley – the first amateur to take nine wickets.

Just one game was played by Rawtenstall in 1917, when there was no league competition, although three regional cup competitions did take place to help clubs raise some well needed revenue. The Maden Cup was competed for by Accrington, Bacup, Church, East Lancashire, Enfield, Haslingden, Ramsbottom and Rawtenstall. Burnley, Lowerhouse, Colne, Nelson and Todmorden competed for the Worsley Cup, whilst Accrington, Church, Enfield, Rishton and East Lancashire fought for the Hacking Cup. The games were played on a league basis but it was not a great success and it was decided to organise just one single Cup Competition in future. In the Maden Cup Rawtenstall played Enfield at home and were skittled out for just 65 runs which they easily passed. Ramsbottom eventually won the final beating Enfield.

For the **1918** season just nine teams were able to compete. Burnley, Nelson, Colne, Lowerhouse and Todmorden were all unable to take part. Indeed not all games were played. 24 players turned out for Rawtenstall in just 13 games in a season which was more about re-building the county, supporting the ill, injured and frail and coming to terms with the senseless loss of so many lives than playing cricket.

Casualties and Fatalities

There was news from the front that popular bowler Jack Kelly had lost a leg whilst fighting. Kelly, from Woodcroft Street, Rawtenstall, had taken over 150 wickets from 1903-1911 with a best of 7-34. Kelly's brother- Thomas was also wounded in the leg and arm at the Dardanelles whilst 36 year old Private James Driver of Cross Farm Cloughfold and the East Lancashire Regiment, a former player in 1903-04, made the supreme sacrifice with news of his death recorded in June 1917. As did Private James Stansfield, the 31 year old died from wounds inflicted. Stansfield played from 1909 -1916 and took over 100 wickets. 18 months earlier he was taking 8-40 at home against Church. Finally news that leading bowler Fred Haworth had also fallen in battle in 1917. Haworth played from 1907 – 1916 taking 226 wickets and scoring nearly 2000 runs. Twelve months earlier he was taking nine wickets at Bacup Road against Burnley. How poignant that his bowling performance still stands as an amateur club record.

A return to a full league programme for **1919** and the re - employment of professionals felt like a return to normality after the chaos and destruction of the last four years. It also saw batsman Alf Pewtress, after serving with the forces, finally invited to play for Lancashire. Now aged 28 he didn't disappoint, scoring 68 against Derbyshire and 86 versus Warwickshire. He also didn't disappoint the Rawtenstall faithful and scored 595 league runs. Fred Barber, who played 5 games for his native Derbyshire, was professional but he only played in 11 matches due to an injury, consequently substitute professionals were found for the other games. It proved to be an encouraging season which also saw Robert Waller take 51 wickets. It was also the third time that the club won the Maden Cup.

	P	W	D	L	Pts	Position
1910	26	6	10	10	22	10/14
1911	26	5	16	5	26	8/14
1912	26	8	9	9	25	9/14
1913	26	7	6	13	20	10/14
1914	**26**	**9**	**12**	**5**	**30**	**4/14**
1915	26	7	8	11	22	11/14
1916	26	5	7	14	17	12/14
1917	*					
1918	13	2	4	7	8	7/9
1919	26	10	8	8	28	6/14

Best season of the decade in bold. * No games played in 1917

1920 - 1929 Makin whoopee

The **1920** season started with Robert Dixon Burrows as professional for the year. The 49 year old Nottinghamshire man had been a county player with Worcestershire for 20 years scoring over 5000 runs and taking just short of 900 wickets. Employed for two years his batting for the club didn't match that of his county. He scored just 409 runs in his two seasons – however with the ball it would be a different story. Against Bacup at Lanehead on 5th June 1920 Rawtenstall had been bowled out for 119. Burrows, bowling right arm fast medium, proceeded to bowl Bacup out for 41 with amazing figures of **10.1 overs, 4 maidens, 11 runs, 9 wickets**. Nearly 100 years later it still stands as the best bowling performance by a Rawtenstall professional or amateur. Despite this feat the club finished bottom of the league losing 17 games, although Burrows was retained for another year.

Even though the Grand Theatre and cinema had not been a success in the town at the end of 1920 the latest cinematic experience was opening in Rawtenstall – The Picture House opened on the 29th December showing "The Rivers End" and "The Cruise of the Make Believes". The seating capacity was 1,309. Films would run in this one big space for the next 55 years. The season of **1921** will be remembered for the show-stopping 71 wickets taken by Tom Waller – an amateur record that stood for nearly 80 years. Waller took 5 wickets or more in an innings six times with a best of 7-22 at Lowerhouse. Brother Bob also chipped in with 46 wickets whilst professional Burrows also took 66 scalps. The batting was led by Pewtress (516) with the Wallers offering some assistance – Tom (296) and Bob (287). It was a significant improvement on the previous season although no-one was prepared for what was to come the following year.

If anyone wanted theatre at its best then The Lancashire League was the place to be in **1922**. The league was set for controversy as the event of the decade and the most controversial since the league's foundation took place. It would go down in the history of Lancashire League cricket as one of the most remarkable and contentious ever. It would of course feature two clubs whose rivalry and competitive spirit have never waned throughout the history of the league. Rawtenstall and Bacup were locked in a battle throughout the season at the top of the table. There was nothing between both sides throughout the whole season and at the end neither team could be separated as they each had the same record.

	Played	W	L	D	Pts
Bacup	26	14	5	7	35
Rawtenstall	26	14	5	7	35

The League Executive came to the conclusion that a play-off game for the title should take place. It occurred at Haslingden's Bent Gate ground where the match would consist of two innings each. The game started on Saturday 16th September but, due to rain, only two and a half hours play was possible. The teams re-assembled again on Monday 18th September for a game which would continue until the 25th and 26th of the month.

The drama and spectacle of the occasion would not do an injustice to a modern day play or film, such was the interest shown throughout the cricketing fraternity of Lancashire. Bacup batted first and scored 142 where professional John Cook took 6 wickets for Rawtenstall. Bacup then disposed of the Rawtenstall team for just 120 with opener Alfred Pewtress scoring 54. Professional for Bacup was Archie Slater who took 4 wickets

The following Saturday the game recommenced. However there was some confusion as the league executive told the clubs that play would end at 6pm, yet told the umpires to try and play the match to a finish. After a new pitch had been prepared, the second innings started and Bacup this time made 155 with Cook taking 6 wickets again. However star batsman Pewtress, who had to travel from Doncaster, had not arrived until Bacup's second innings had been completed. He was told by the Bacup captain Jimmy Midgely Snr that he would not be allowed to bat!

Rawtenstall threatened to abandon the game so the objection was withdrawn. Rawtenstall needed 185 to win – however controversy would reign again at 6pm when Rawtenstall had made 113 for 7. Pewtress the potential match winner was still there 48 not out when the Rawtenstall captain Johnson Moore went out on to the field and called his batsmen back in. The 5000 crowd present were not only amazed at this but, as you can imagine, 'somewhat annoyed'.

Both teams were ordered to re-appear the following Monday at 4pm to conclude the game. Another large crowd had turned up to see which way the match would go. Rawtenstall hopes were pinned on Pewtress and Bacup just needed 3 wickets. The crowd waited with bated breath for the teams to take the field but.... Bacup hadn't turned up! A six hour emergency league committee meeting took place on the Wednesday evening and the outcome was to pronounce both teams as joint winners of the league. The cup would remain in the hands of the league and no medals would be awarded!

The Rawtenstall captain was reprimanded and the club fined £20 (£585). Bacup were fined £50 (£1,460) for their "Grave and deliberate action."

Back Row: P Carr (scorer) J Cook (pro) S Haworth, R Waller, JH Woodcock, T Waller, GR Fenton, WE Ashworth (secretary)
Front Row: H Nuttall, G Ashworth, J Moore (capt) A Taylor, AW Pewtress

The Rawtenstall team that played against Bacup in the 1922 Play-Off

45

Below is the record of Alfred Pewtress for Rawtenstall and Lancashire. Had the war not intervened on his career who knows how many more appearances he could have made for his club and County.

Alfred William Pewtress Born: 27th August 1891, Rawtenstall.
Died: 21st September 1960, Brighton, Sussex, England.

Lancashire League Career Batting & Fielding for Rawtenstall (1908-1931)

M	I	NO	Runs	HS	Ave	100	50	Ct
250	249	23	5369	122*	23.75	2	28	92

First-Class Career Batting & Fielding for Lancashire (1919-1925)

M	I	NO	Runs	HS	Ave	100	50	Ct
50	73	5	1483	89	21.80	0	7	16

There was additional success for the club as the second eleven were league champions for the second time. However, such was the ill-feeling and bad taste felt by both sides and the supporters of both teams regarding the first eleven it was felt that the season, the game and the outcome be put to the back of the memories of all concerned. One statistic that is worth noting is that the four Rossendale Valley clubs created a record by finishing in the top four positions. This was the first time that clubs from one area had achieved this.

The **1923** season was less controversial with Tom Waller making 351 runs. Three bowlers took all but 17 of the total number of wickets. Leading the way was professional John Cook with 77. Preston based Cook was one of four brothers to become league professionals, three of whom also represented Lancashire. Brother Lawrence would be sub professional the following season. The two amateur bowlers taking the wickets were George Ashworth (42) and Tom Waller (41).

Further leisure opportunities were being created in the valley – the latest being Rossendale Male Voice Choir which was founded in 1924 by Fred Tomlinson MBE. He was instrumental in moulding young men from the valley into one of the country's finest male voice choirs winning many competitions including the International Eisteddfod in Llangollen, Wales.

There would be plenty for the Rawtenstall faithful to sing about in two years' time but it wasn't in the season of **1924**, certainly not in the case of the first eleven. Bertie Francis Morgan was employed as professional who had played six first class games for Somerset. His career at Rawtenstall was even less brief! He lasted just four games before being replaced by 40 year old Lawrence Cook.

Cook was no stranger to the valley and to Bacup folk in particular as he was also a footballer and scored the winning goal for Bacup FC in their Lancashire Junior Cup triumph in 1911. No-one scored over 300 runs although George Ashworth took 50 wickets. The second team though won their championship again after the previous success in 1922.

Rawtenstall Junior League Champions 1924

There was even less to sing and dance about in **1925** despite the performances of Yorkshireman Ernest Smith, who came recommended as a bowler who could bat a bit. Smith (1888 –1972) played sixteen matches for Yorkshire County Cricket Club from 1914 to 1926. He also played for Colne in the league (1921-1924) Born in Barnsley, Smith was a right-handed batsman and a slow left arm medium pace bowler.

He was top scorer in 1925 with 368 runs which demonstrated where Rawtenstall needed to focus its attention. Maybe debutant 15 year old Reg Hitch might be one to watch. The bowling of Smith though was incredible. He acquired 119 wickets in his first season including 12 x 5+ wicket hauls. His figures of 9-19 against Lowerhouse, 9-43 against Ramsbottom and 9-45 against Todmorden – were all at Rawtenstall. He also had three 8 wicket hauls. Amazingly Rawtenstall finished third from the bottom of the league having lost far too many games. Clearly with Smith providing the ammunition with the ball it just needed backing up with some strong batting performances and who knows what could happen.

So as **1926** approached there was a degree of anticipation amongst the Bacup Road faithful. They wouldn't be disappointed as 17 year old Reg Hitch (534) led the way with the bat well supported by four other amateurs (Harold Clegg, Joey Middleton, JE Downes and Tom Waller) who each scored over 250 runs. Hitch would go on to become one of the clubs leading amateur batsmen scoring over 5000 runs over two decades. Professional Smith also contributed 365 runs but it was his bowling that would be critical to winning the championship. His 111 wickets were nearly an exact repeat of the previous season. Again he had 12 x 5 plus wicket games including 3 eight -wicket hauls. Amateur Tom Waller also took the plaudits with 54 wickets including a best ever 7-10 at Enfield who were bowled out for just 26! Only one game was lost all season and the championship was won by four points.

There was good news off the field as well as the Annual Report produced in December 1926 showed a £90 (£3,700) profit for the season, whose recent bazaar effort yielded net proceeds amounting to £2,419. (£100,000). The ordinary income, which totalled £1,209, (£50,000), included gate receipts of £740 (£30,000) and members' subscriptions (including arrears) of £356 (£14,600). On the expenditure side the main items were: wages £352, match expenses £156, talent money £35 and repairs to ground £209.

Ground purchase falls through.

Just as celebrations were coming to an end came the news in October that attempts to purchase the ground had fallen through. Harry Whitehead JP was in discussions with Greenbank Estate Company, who owned the land, to purchase it for £2000 (£83,000 today). In a letter to the Rossendale Free Press on 9th October Mr Whitehead outlined in detail how negotiations had been ongoing for a period of 6 months. Initially the figure had been accepted although it appears that through various correspondence conditions were being applied by the Greenbank Company – in particular no cricket buildings to be built in some areas of the plan. Consequently the purchase fell through although work would continue to take place on securing the ground on a permanent basis.

The year of **1927** saw the third year of Smith at Bacup Road. Expectations were high after the previous year's success. The batting again wasn't particularly impressive. Reg Hitch with 310 and Harold Clegg with 305 were the only ones past the 300 mark. It was particularly embarrassing in the game at Colne on 7th May when Rawtenstall were all out for 23! Smith couldn't repeat his 100 wickets although 83, including nine 5 wicket hauls, was very good. The positive news from the bowling front came from youngster Norman Coupe who took 39 wickets in his first full season including 6-18 at Church helping to bowl them out for 29. A mid – table finish was as good as it got.

Back Row: Harold Clegg, Robert Waller, Reg Hitch, JE Downes, Tom Waller Jnr

Front Row: Ernest Smith (pro), George Holt (capt), Albert Taylor, Tom Waller. Kneeling - Harold Whitehead, Joey Middleton,

Rawtenstall League Champions 1926

49

Back Row: Peter Carr (scorer) Tom Waller Jr, Robert Waller, H Whitehead JP (President) Harold Clegg, H Longworth (League representative), Tom Waller, Reg Hitch, R Tomlinson (secretary)

Front Row: JE Downes, Ernest Smith (Pro), George Richard Holt (capt), Albert E Taylor, Joey Middleton, H Whitehead.

Rawtenstall League Champions 1926

A teenager was causing quite a stir in the club in **1928**. The 13 year old made his debut for the second eleven on 2nd June. A year later on 27th July 1929 he was making his debut for the first team – his name was Winston Place, more from him later. Smith (right) completed his stint as professional with another century of wickets (107) and thirteen 5+wicket matches. He would certainly be a hard act to replace. Hitch and Middleton both scored over 300 and Fred Pewtress notched 269 in just nine games.

Year	Balls	Mdns	Runs	Wkts	Best	Ave	5+ w innings	Strike Rate	Econ
1925	2836	115	1064	119	9-19	8.94	12	23.83	2.25
1926	2720	137	868	111	8-18	7.81	12	24.50	1.91
1927	2623	124	860	83	7-31	10.36	9	31.60	1.96
1928	2818	107	1099	107	8-43	10.27	13	26.33	2.33

Ernest Smith bowling record for Rawtenstall

It was another club that set the crowds flooding to the grounds hours before games started in **1929**. The club was Nelson and the reason was a young man from the small island of Trinidad in the West Indies. He would put the league on the map not just within Lancashire and England but across the world. His name was Learie Constantine. This year the batting came good for Rawtenstall - Reg Hitch (539) including a best of 97, was well supported by Harold Clegg (460), George Hargreaves (328) and Joey Middleton (324). Professional J William Sunderland (248) provided more potency with the ball taking 80 wickets including 8-29 at home to Haslingden.

	Played	W	D	L	Pts	Position
1920	26	4	5	17	13	14/14
1921	26	9	7	10	25	9/14
***1922**	**26**	**14**	**7**	**5**	**35**	**1/14**
1923	26	7	10	9	24	7/14
1924	26	8	11	7	27	6/14
1925	26	6	4	16	16	12/14
1926	**26**	**16**	**9**	**1**	**41**	**1/14**
1927	26	8	10	8	26	7/14
1928	26	6	11	9	23	11/14
1929	26	5	12	9	22	11/14

Best seasons of the decade in bold * tied with Bacup

1930 - 1939 In the mood

Rawtenstall engaged Percy Sharples (below) as their professional for the **1930** season. The 25 year old right hand batsman and slow left arm orthodox spinner from Oldham managed just 173 runs and a top score of 38. There was little support from the amateurs apart from Reg Hitch. Sharples fared better with the ball taking 69 wickets and a best of 8-38 in a match that was lost at East Lancashire's Alexandra Meadows ground. Only two games were won and it would be the worst possible start to the decade. In the Worsley Cup first round tie at Haslingden, Rawtenstall batting first could only score 78 and 30 of those were made by 16 year old opener Winston Place making his debut in the competition. Haslingden edged their way to the total but professional Sharples had other ideas and took 6-36. Haslingden were all out for 76 and Rawtenstall had won by just two runs.

Many acknowledge that the first professional to acquire star status was Sydney Barnes. Barnes (right) played in the League from 1895 - 1905 and then from 1931 - 1933. He started his professional career at Rishton from 1895 -1899, after which he had two seasons at Burnley and Church respectively. He was professional at Burnley when Archie C. MacLaren, hearing of his skill, invited him to the nets at Old Trafford. "He thumped me on the left thigh. He hit my gloves from a length. He actually said, `Sorry, sir!' and I said, `don't be sorry, Barnes. You're coming to Australia with me.'"

MacLaren on the strength of a net practice with Barnes chose him for his England team in Australia in 1901-02. In the first Test of that rubber, Barnes took five for 65 in 35.1 overs, and one for 74 in 16 overs. In the second Test he took six for 42 and seven for 121 and bowled 80 six-ball overs in this game.

He broke down with a leg strain in the third Test and could bowl no more for MacLaren, who, winning the first Test and now without Barnes, lost the next four games of the rubber.

Barnes' test record of 189 victims stood as a record for over 30 years. In his last four test matches in South Africa in 1913/14 he took 49 wickets! By the time he became Rawtenstall's professional in 1931 he would be 58 years of age. The previous season the club had finished bottom of the league and the Bacup Road faithful needed a star performer to turn to.

1931 nearly saw arguably the greatest ever batsmen enter the league. Accrington offered Australian, Donald Bradman, terms. Another league legend Learie Constantine had asked Bradman if he would be interested in playing in the Lancashire League. He had been offered £600 (£27,500) for 30 matches - £150 talent money (collections) and £150 for exhibition matches. A rough total today would be the equivalent of £41,000 a year! Oh how clubs today would dream of having those financial resources available to them. The contract was for two years and the other bonus quoted was "no ground work" although £2 per week would need to be paid for board. The reply from Bradman to the secretary of Accrington was short sweet and with class ... "Regret decline your offer. Appreciate pleasant nature of negotiations"- Bradman.

The year also saw a remarkable performance by wicketkeeper Jack W Barnes. In the match at Enfield on 1st August, Barnes took six victims including 5 stumped. The Enfield card read "stumped Barnes bowled Barnes" three times, as both worked their magic in tandem. Two batting performances stood out in the season. Joey Middleton made his first century (102) for the club in the home game against Enfield where Barnes also took eight wickets and on 7th July, 17 year old Winston Place made his first 50 for the club, 51 not out at home against Rishton.

1932 saw the opening of the Astoria Ballroom in the town with 700 dancers attending the Rawtenstall British Legion Ball. Sydney Barnes was also having a ball taking another 100+ wickets. Batsman Middleton, who was now captain, scored

506 runs and another home century (101 not out) against Enfield. He even chipped in with 20 wickets in a season where Barnes excelled 9-20 at home to Burnley, 8-28 at home and 8-43 away to Lowerhouse. In the game at Nelson, Barnes took 7-30 and Nelson with Constantine out for just 3 runs, were all out for 67. The Trinidad man came back with a vengeance, out-performing Barnes taking 8-24 seven of which were clean bowled. Rawtenstall were all out for 59 and Nelson again took the Championship.

CLR James of the Manchester Guardian described the duel between Constantine and Barnes:

"So the pair watched one another like two fencers sparring for an opening. The crowd sat tense, was this recitative suddenly to burst into the melody of fours and sixes? The Nelson crowd at least hoped so, but it was not to be. Some insignificant trundler at the other end, who bowled mediocre balls, bowled Constantine with one of them (the insignificant trundler was Norman Coupe). *When Barnes came in, Constantine was hurling the ball violently through the air, Barnes was older than Constantine's father and the wicket was faster now. He stayed there some forty minutes for 10 but Constantine bowled him behind his back. He came in slowly amidst the plaudits of the Nelson crowd, applauding his innings and their satisfaction at him having been dismissed".*

Barnes though did manage 10 more league wickets than Constantine.

The year also saw the end of the tramway system in Rawtenstall. Who would have thought that 80 years later they would be introducing them again in our major cities and towns.

Barnes was back on track for his last season with the club in **1933.** He was now nearly 60 years old and in a season where no batsman, other than Joey Middleton, scored more than 300 runs. However the year did see the first century made by Reg Hitch, 101 at Accrington. The bowling too was disappointing, Barnes only took 54 wickets including 9-53 at Ramsbottom and still ending up on the losing side! Only one game was won all season and unsurprisingly Rawtenstall occupied bottom position in the league. It was a sad way for Barnes to finish his time at the club but his statistics will always stand.

Year	Balls	Mdns	Runs	Wkts	B B	Ave	5 wkt	S/R	Econ
1931	2021	94	725	115	8-24	6.30	15	17.57	2.15
1932	2642	159	819	113	9-20	7.24	12	23.38	1.85
1933	1646	62	746	54	9-55	13.81	4	30.48	2.71

Sydney Barnes at Rawtenstall, his average for 1931 remains a club record

1934 will be remembered for 20 year old Winston Place's first century for the club. It occurred on the 9th June at home against Ramsbottom. Place scored 111 not out in a match that ended in a draw. There were many centurions to savour that year, not only Constantine at Nelson but his West Indian team mate George Headley was also racking them up at Haslingden. James Patrick McNally was the Rawtenstall paid man - a South African who batted left hand and bowled right arm off spinners but he wasn't in the same class with just 328 runs and 69 wickets including 7-38 at home against Church. The amateur batsmen though had a good year with Place leading the way with 645 runs followed by Bob Howarth (483), Middleton (453) and Hargreaves (425). Amateur bowler Geoffrey Wint matched professional McNally with a career best 69 wickets, including 7-16 off eleven overs at home to East Lancashire in which he also performed a hat-trick, only the second amateur to do so. With such strong performances a 6th place was achieved.

A new tea pavilion with terracing below was erected at a cost of £500 (£25,500) 'The cup that cheers but does not inebriate' was somewhat prophetic as Rawtenstall overcame Bacup for the first time in a Worsley Cup game. Chasing 184 a match- winning 72 from Place saw the Bacup Road men home.

There was though controversy in the two league games against Haslingden. The first fixture at Bent Gate saw the Haslingden professional George Headley score 125 in a Haslingden total of 244-6. Rawtenstall were never going to chase this total in such a limited time so the batsmen and particularly the tail blocked delivery after delivery. So annoyed with this Headley sent down an underarm ball which was resented by many of the Rawtenstall fans as an act of unsportsmanlike behaviour. However the return fixture caused even more controversy. Haslingden had been dismissed for 160. In reply Rawtenstall were up against the clock and were 160-9 when at 7pm prompt the umpires removed the stumps to call time. Part of the crowd surged onto the field and surrounded the umpires and police were summoned. The aftermath was reported in the Lancashire Evening Post.

UMPIRES CENSURED. SEQUEL TO RECENT MATCH AT RAWTENSTALL. Stormy scenes at Rawtenstall cricket ground a few weeks ago were investigated at Accrington on Wednesday night by the Lancashire League Committee. The umpires drew stumps when Rawtenstall had equalled Haslingden's total with one wicket standing. The umpires, who were censured, said that they had not seen the lost time displayed on the score box, but the committee agreed that it had been adequately displayed. It was decided that the result of the match should remain a tie, and the Rawtenstall club were recommended to display the lost-time board more prominently.

Rawtenstall turned to another elder statesman in **1935** and one who again had a pedigree of success in the Lancashire League - Archibald Gilbert Slater.

His career spanned from 1911 to 1941. He made his first class debut for Derbyshire in June 1911. After the war he played County Cricket in 1919 and 1921 but did not return till 1927. In-between he was professional for Bacup from 1921 to 1926, and played in the infamous Championship play off decider against Rawtenstall in 1922. Slater returned to Derbyshire in 1927 and his last game for them was in 1931. He then returned to the Lancashire League and had three seasons at Colne, 1932 -34, before arriving at Rawtenstall. Now in his mid-40's, could Slater (pictured right when professional for Bacup) still perform? It didn't take long to find out and oh... the irony. The game in question was the derby at home to Bacup. Slater skittled the Lanehead men out for just 40 runs and took 8-21.

Slater ended up taking 89 league wickets with eight 5+wicket hauls. Joey Middleton chipped in with 38 scalps including 7-72 at home to Enfield.

Place (756) led with the bat followed by Slater (564), Reg Hitch (532) and Bob Howarth (354). With Slater contracted for the following season the Rawtenstall faithful felt that a championship or even the cup was within reach.

They weren't far wrong but it would be bridesmaid's day in **1936.** Slater was now 46 but he galvanised the team in to runners up spot in the league and the Worsley Cup. The team were now without their talisman batsman Place who was playing minor counties games for Lancashire second eleven. Reg Hitch led the way with 538 including a century (105) at home to Accrington. Slater made 434, Howarth 395 and George Hargreaves 371. Slater took 71 wickets including 9-45 at home against Church and 8-22 again at home against Ramsbottom. Norman Coupe with 33 wickets and 5-12 at Enfield was a good foil for Slater. The top of the table clash at home to Nelson recorded a gate of £242 (£12,250) however torrential rain caused an abandonment of the match. It was Nelson's championship though by only two points. In the cup, victories over Haslingden and Ramsbottom included a hat-trick for Norman Coupe in the game at Acre Bottom.

The semi-final tie was at Burnley. Rawtenstall batted first but could only make 131. However Burnley could only make 97. Slater took 5-35 and Rawtenstall had finally made the Worsley Cup final. It took place on 25th and 26th August at home. Accrington scored 198 with Wint taking 4-45. However the Rawtenstall batsmen couldn't get going. Four players were out in their 20's and Accrington won by 38 runs. The good news was the report that financially the season was one of their most successful. Income totalled £1,692 (£86,000), expenditure £1,403 which included the purchase of a motor mower for £92. Of the surplus of £288 a sum of £261 was written off as depreciation, leaving a net profit of £26 (£1,320). Gate receipts, including £173 from the Worsley Cup games, amounted to £896 (£45,500) and £198 was received from insurance of gates.

The Palace Cinema closed in 1936 although it re-opened at Christmas with pantomime and variety shows and in January 1937, the Crawshawbooth Operatic Society staged Gilbert & Sullivan's "The Mikado". Slater was still the 'Yeoman of the Guard' at Bacup Road and season **1937** was his best with the bat scoring 571 runs. Reg Hitch was top scorer with 581 and Middleton wasn't far behind with 493 including 101 not out at home to Haslingden. There was another centurion too - George Hargreaves 102 not out at home against Church. Hargreaves (352) and Howarth (324) also contributed well to the cause. Bowling - wise, Slater (71), Harold Hannah (30), including 5-17 at Burnley, and Middleton (25) enabled a third position to be reached. The year also saw Winston Place make his full debut for Lancashire playing in 14 games and scoring his first of many centuries.

Slater's last season was in **1938** and he only managed to play in 16 games but still acquired 404 runs and 33 wickets. Encouragement came from amateur bowlers Ross Taylor (36 including 7-25 at home to Enfield) and Norman Coupe (35). George Hargreaves was leading scorer with 425 including 101 not out at Rishton. Hitch, Middleton and Howarth all scored over 300 but too many drawn games ensured a lower half league position.

Slater packed his bag after four very good seasons, steady with the bat but very accomplished with the ball. His record is highlighted below.

Batting	M	I	N/O	R	H/S	Ave	50's	Cat
League	91	82	14	1973	90	29	12	36
Cup	9	8	2	212	72*	35	2	3
Bowling	Balls	M	R	Wkts	Best	Ave	5 W	Econ
League	8288	355	3305	267	9-45	12	23	2.39
Cup	1321	67	423	33	5-35	13	3	1.92

Back: Umpire (unknown), A Bannister, Ross Taylor, Reg Hitch, V Whittaker, Geoffrey Wint, Unknown,

Front: Robert C Howarth, Norman Coupe, Jack W Barnes, Archie Slater (pro) Billy Cowell, George Hargreaves, AW Pewtress

Seated: Joey Middleton, J Whitehead.

Rawtenstall League & Worsley Cup Runners Up 1936

As **1939** arrived attentions were diverted to what was happening across the English Channel. Closer to home the footwear industry in the valley was now employing over 6000 people. However there was nothing shoddy about the reputation of Rawtenstall's professional for the year. Victor James Evans had played 62 matches for Essex from 1932-37 and had taken 129 wickets.

Nevertheless the 27 year old like many other professionals at that time struggled with the bat making just 227 runs. With the ball though, the right arm off break bowler took 72 wickets, including 8-35 in a victory at Colne. Harold Hannah had his best season with the ball (51) including 7-15 at home to Enfield six of which were clean bowled.

As tight a finish as you could expect took place on 27th June in the home fixture against Todmorden. Batting first Rawtenstall declared on 189-8 with Norman Coupe making his first 50 for the club. In reply Todmorden looked to be coasting with both openers Scott and Crowther scoring 50s. However wickets began to fall and with 5 minutes left Todmorden still required 12 runs to win. The scores were level, Todmorden were 189-8 but their professional Macaulay was caught off the last ball and the game was a tie.

In the Worsley Cup a short trip to Haslingden in the first round saw Harold Hannah take 5-25 in dismissing the Bent Gate side for 124. However Rawtenstall couldn't even make three figures and were bowled out for just 83, Evans top scoring with 32.

	P	W	D	L	Pts	Position
1930	26	2	12	12	16	14/14
1931	26	9	13	4	31	5/14
1932	26	8	11	7	27	6/14
1933	26	1	16	9	18	14/14
1934	26	8	11	7	27	6/14
1935	26	8	10	8	26	8/14
1936	**26**	**12**	**11**	**3**	**47**	**2/14**
1937	26	12	9	5	45	3/14
1938	26	6	14	6	32	10/14
1939	26	7	9	10	30	9/14

Best season of the decade in bold

1940 - 1949 Rum and Coca Cola

The old adage that cricket is a 'team game' was never more apparent than at the start of the decade. Teams again were without professionals and would remain so until 1945. As with the previous war campaign many men signed up although cricket continued to be played throughout.

A runners-up spot started the decade off and four bowlers shared the majority of the wickets - Robert Banks (38), Norman Coupe (35), Ross Taylor (34) and Joey Middleton (32). Banks took a career best 8-16 at Todmorden. On the batting front George Hoyle (445), Robert Howarth (406) Joey Middleton (405) and George Hargreaves (355) ensured that the 'Team Effort' would be rewarded.

1941 saw Hargie Greenwood score his first century, 122 not out against Burnley and George Hargreaves also hit a century (131) at home to Enfield but both were slightly overshadowed by Middleton's 166 not out at home against Bacup. It was the highest individual score in the league by some distance. Nearly 80 years later it remains the third highest score ever made by a Rawtenstall player. Norman Coupe hit 569 runs and Middleton 624. Harold Hannah took 45 wickets and Bob Banks 33 but despite all these impressive performances, it was a bottom half season in the end.

The following year was a slight improvement. Middleton (right) was leading the way *again* with the bat with 428 runs and another century (125) *again* at home and *again* against Bacup. He also took 48 wickets (6-12) his best figures at home to Rishton. Norman Coupe just out-performed Middleton taking 52 scalps. Thirty three men played for the first eleven over the course of the season so consistency was always going to be difficult but, considering many men were signing up for more taxing challenges abroad, the willingness and resolve of the men who played has to be acknowledged.

1943 saw another good all round performance by Joey Middleton firstly taking 49 wickets including 7-49 at Accrington and scoring 342 runs – rather a modest total considering his record. H Derrick also hit 332 whilst Steve Wells took 35 wickets and 7-26 away against Church. The best bowling figures came from Norman Coupe who in his 20 wickets for the season took 8-35 of them at home to Ramsbottom. Another mid-table finish was where the team would end up.

The least said about **1944** the better. Just one victory all season and unsurprisingly, finishing at the bottom of the league. Middleton didn't play that year and the only real highlight was a reasonable all round performance from Jimmy Warburton with 341 runs and 33 wickets, and 326 from W Telfer. This time thirty seven players turned out for the club.

The following year saw the re-introduction of professionals and for Rawtenstall a marked improvement. Leslie John Todd (left) was the first Professional engaged for **1945**. Todd played for Kent CCC prior to the war and after it (1927 -1950). During the war he served in the RAF. A 'leftie' medium pace bowler/off spinner and middle order bat he looked and sounded exactly like the type of player to flourish in the league. He finished second in the league batting averages with 512 runs from 17 innings and with 42 wickets, including 7-55 in an all-round display at home against Haslingden where he also carried his bat, winning the game with 67 not out. With no other batsman scoring over 200 runs and no other bowler taking more than 20 wickets you would have thought he would be worth re-engaging however his attitude and temperament was described as "a nightmare to handle." Nevertheless, a fifth place after finishing the previous season bottom with just one win would be a significant improvement.

In February **1946** the town was recovering from a disastrous fire (right), which destroyed the indoor market and shops.

A few months later the Rawtenstall faithful were recovering from the exploits of their latest professional. Another new nationality graced the Bacup Road.

Thomas J Bartley was born in Wales and represented Cheshire in the Minor Counties Championship. He was engaged by Rawtenstall for just one year and the 38 year old probably registered the worst ever batting performance by a Rawtenstall professional in the history of the club. In the 21 matches he played he scored just 31 runs in 10 innings with a top score of 11 not out and average of 7! He did though manage to take 31 wickets.

His fame would come later in life as he became a first class umpire and stood in 6 home test matches from 1954-1956. Jimmy Warburton (458) was top scorer in a season that finished mid table. The consolation was that, after a twenty two year gap, the second eleven were winning their championship for the third time.

Rawtenstall Junior League Champions 1946

Back Row: N Whittaker, H Collinge (scorer), G Whittaker (president) R Tomlinson (secretary), E Ashworth.

Standing: R Banks, R Whalley, M Howarth, T Kidd, H Hannah, T Incles.

Seated: J Throup, B Longworth (capt), G Hargreaves, W Shackleton.

Front: K Barnes, WB Haughton, G Nuttall.

Rumours were spreading across the town that the Rawtenstall committee were to splash the cash and sign legendary Australian all-rounder Keith Miller as their professional for 1947. It proved only to be just that.... a rumour. There was no doubt that the Rawtenstall committee needed to find a better quality professional for **1947** – and they did in securing the services of another Australian - 22 year old Kenneth James Grieves.

Grieves was born in Sydney, and moved to England in 1947 where he pursued a football career. He played for Bury, Bolton Wanderers and Stockport County, making a total of 147 Football League appearances as a goalkeeper between 1947 and 1958. He was an "all-rounder" in all senses of the term as in his first season with Rawtenstall he hit 908 runs with good support from Tommy Incles (498) George Hoyle (393) and Hargie Greenwood (371). He also took 89 wickets supported by Edward Poole (38).

It was one of the hotter summers on record and Grieves made the most of the good conditions. History has a reputation of repeating itself and for Rawtenstall it did in the most heart breaking of ways.

It would be 'nearly- men' again for the team just as in 1936 when they finished runners up in both the league and Worsley Cup. After a first round victory over Ramsbottom, Haslingden came to Bacup Road for the second round tie. Rawtenstall, batting first, could only score 104. However the Bentgate men were skittled out for just 39. No-one reached double figures with Edward Poole taking 5-15 and Grieves 5-13 ... all bowled!

They faced Nelson in the semi-final and in a nail biting encounter Rawtenstall made 130 -7 with wicketkeeper Jimmy Warburton scoring 40 not out. Grieves (left) then took 5-43 as Nelson were all out for 115.

The final at home to East Lancashire saw Rawtenstall fail again with the bat being all out for just 91.The Blackburn men won easily by 6 wickets. However, as you can imagine, the Rawtenstall faithful quickly acknowledged that they had 'a gud un' and Grieves was signed up for the next year.

Rawtenstall League and Cup Runners Up 1947

Back: K Bradshaw, H Greenwood, K Grieves (pro), S Wells, N Coupe, K Barnes.

Front: E Poole, J Warburton, G Hoyle (capt), T Incles, J Middleton.

The **1948** season saw the debut of a young 16 year old wicketkeeper from Cloughfold by the name of John Jordan (right). He would continue to keep wicket for the club for the next 5 years, but would eventually attract the interest of the County.

Grieves provided a true all round display of his talent in the game at Haslingden on 3rd July. He firstly hit his one and only century for the club (119) then took 7-34 – six of which were bowled and the seventh caught and bowled! Grieves scored a modest 529 runs for the season. Incles (357) was the other main contributor. Grieves took 83 wickets with good support from Bob Banks (42) and Steve Wells (32). Fifth place brought with it news that

Greives was off to Lancashire for a career that was to blossom and flourish throughout the 1950s and 60s. In Greaves 16 year career with the county he captained them in 1963 and 1964. A middle order batsman, he made 452 first class appearances for Lancashire and made a county record 555 catches. Grieves often fielded at first slip and in 1951, he took eight catches in a match against Sussex, six of them in one innings. He scored over 20,000 runs for the county and is eighth all-time record scorer.

Another Rawtenstall and Lancashire player was also in the news in 1948. Winston Place (back row second left) was touring the Caribbean with the England Test Team.

1949 not only brought with it one of the warmest summers for many a year but also the third runner up spot in the decade. For many it would provide the opportunity to see some of the finest cricketers to ever grace the Lancashire League. At Bacup was Everton Weekes, Colne had Bill Alley, at Burnley was Cec Pepper and at Rawtenstall one of the all-time greats would be appearing at Bacup Road. It would be the first time that the Rawtenstall committee had ventured to the sub-continent of India to secure a paid man. Was it a risk worth taking? Well the unsuspecting crowds of Bacup Road would be in for a treat as they were truly entertained by the quiet unassuming nature of Vijay Samuel Hazare. Hazare (1915 –2004) was from the state of Maharashtra in India. He captained the Indian cricket team in 14 matches between 1951 and 1953. In India's 25th Test match he led them to their first ever Test victory against England at Madras. Hazare was one of eight children born in a working-class family in Sangli, Maharashtra.

Primarily a right-hand batsman, Hazare (below), was also a right-hand medium-pace bowler. A "shy, retiring" man (according to Wisden in 1952); it was widely thought that he was not a natural captain and that his batting suffered as a result.

Hazare's Test record speaks for itself: he amassed 2,192 runs in 30 Test matches with a batting average of 47.65. His first-class record is even more impressive, with a batting average of 58.38 for his 18,740 runs (highest first-class aggregate for an Indian player after Sunil Gavaskar, Sachin Tendulkar and Rahul Dravid). He scored 60 first-class centuries (including 7 in Tests). His bowling record was more modest, and he took 595 first-class wickets (including 20 in Tests, and Donald Bradman's wicket three times) at a bowling average of 24.61.

John Arlott described him thus:

"Tiger hunter, all round cricketer and captain in the state army of Baroda looks, at first encounter, none of these things. A slim man with a shy, gentle smile, much averse to walking in the rain, hiding himself within himself at social functions, rarely speaking unless spoken to, one would take the impression of an impractical recluse". However on the field he was a different character and revered opponent. In 1949 he acquired 15 collections in 22 games totalling £158 (nearly £5000).

The year also saw the retirement of amateur batsman Joey Middleton just before the Bacup game on 18th June. The ground was packed to the rafters, as you can see in the picture overleaf, creating a £345 gate (£10,800). "The little man with the bat" as he was known to many signed off with 7330 runs including the highest individual score for an amateur (166 not out), 5 centuries and 25 fifties. The Bacup players, including professional and league legend Everton Weekes, and even the umpires applauded him to the wicket. The game was filmed and recorded and is available via the North West Film Archive based at Manchester Metropolitan University. The club wanted to provide Middleton with a retirement gift for his dedicated service and suggested a target of 7,330 pennies – one for every run that he had scored. The public responded far better and 14,203 pennies ensured Joey received a cheque for £251 (£7,800).

Joey Middleton Lancashire League Batting, Bowling & Fielding (1921-1949)

M	I	NO	Runs	HS	Ave	100	50	Ct	St
447	414	62	7330	166*	20.82	5	25	152	1

Balls	Mdns	Runs	Wkts	BB	Ave	5wI	Strike Rate	Econ
14760	265	7492	439	7-49	17.06	16	33.62	3.04

Rawtenstall League Runners Up 1949

Back: T Incles, N Coupe, H Greenwood, D Whittaker, S Wells, D Banks.

Front: J Jordan, J Middleton, B Longworth (capt), V Hazarre (pro), K Barnes.

Crowd scenes from 1949

The picture above is taken in the late 1940's from Ilex Mill just before the old pavilion is replaced. Alder Grange School can be seen in the top left.

	Played	W	D	L	Pts	Position
1940	**26**	**12**	**11**	**3**	**47**	**2/14**
1941	26	6	8	8	26	10/14
1942	26	6	5	11	29	7/14
1943	26	6	7	9	27	8/14
1944	26	1	16	5	8	14/14
1945	26	6	4	12	24	5/14
1946	26	7	13	6	34	7/14
1947	**26**	**15**	**8**	**3**	**53**	**2/14**
1948	26	10	10	6	40	5/14
1949	**26**	**13**	**11**	**2**	**50**	**2/14**

Best seasons of the decade in bold

1950 - 1959 Memories are made of this

If cricket fans thought 1949 was fielded with star studied world class cricket Professionals then the 1950s had them all. Spectators from the 14 Lancashire League clubs would be treated to some of the finest players to ever grace the game. After the sun of 1949 came 1950 which was one of the wettest summers on record, but clubs in the Lancashire League were making the most of the responses from the local community who were keen and eager to watch their local teams. Rawtenstall was no exception to this with gates of up to 10,000 people cramming into Bacup Road during the 1950s. That's quite amazing when you consider that the population of the town in 1951 was just over 25,000. With a membership of 3000, facilities would need to be improved. It was the players and umpires who benefitted first with a new pavilion built in 1951 at an estimated cost of £5,000 (£156,000). Perhaps it was justified as a response to finishing runners up for the 1950 season.

Out with the old (above) and in with the new (below)

The decade started off very positively largely due to the performances of the new Australian professional George Edward Tribe (1920 - 2009). Tribe was a left-hand batsman and slow left-arm orthodox and 'chinaman' bowler. Tribe played with great success for Victoria

69

State immediately after the Second World War, taking 86 wickets in just 13 games. He also played in three Tests under Donald Bradman in the 1946-47 Ashes series.

In 1947 Tribe (left) joined Milnrow in the Central Lancashire League and took 136 scalps in his first season. He followed that performance with a record 148 wickets the following year. In 1950 having reached 30 years of age, he joined Rawtenstall for two seasons.

What an impact he had! Many people at the time and many afterwards argued that he was one of the best professionals the club had ever had. It wasn't just the 'George Tribe Show' in 1950 as two amateurs scored centuries. Kevin Read (107 not out), at Enfield in his only century for the club. It was a game which also saw Steve Wells take a career best 7-11, including four wickets in four balls to bowl Enfield out for just 40. Hargie Greenwood (103 not out) scored his second 'ton' in a win at Accrington where Tribe took 8-40. Reid (546) Incles (389) and Greenwood (381) supported Tribe (646) with the bat whilst Tribe's 107 wickets and 50 for Steve Wells were the cream of the bowling.

History repeated itself again for the third time as Rawtenstall finished in second place and just 3 points behind champions Burnley and runners up for the third time in the Worsley Cup after victories over Ramsbottom, Bacup and Todmorden. This time the final was against Burnley. Cec Pepper, Burnley's Australian professional, won the battle of the Australian pros taking 6-54. Rawtenstall made just 107 and Burnley won by 8 wickets.

1951 was practically a repeat of the previous year with Tribe making 791 runs including his highest score of 92 not out. The amateur batting was giving him plenty of support with Incles (521), Kenny Barnes (480,) Greenwood (359) and Philip White (307) contributing. Tribe (105) and Wells (42) provided the ammunition with the ball. Equal third alongside Todmorden and Rawtenstall were maintaining their consistency of being a top five club for the previous five years.

Rawtenstall League & Cup Runners Up 1950

Back: G Hargreaves, K Reid, T Incles, S Wells, G Hoyle, K Barnes.

Seated: F Riding, N Coupe, B Longworth (Capt), GE Tribe (pro), WB Haughton.

Tribe was an engineer by trade and he joined a Northamptonshire based firm in 1951. His prolific record saw Northamptonshire offer him terms for that season and he proved an immediate success. Tribe played for the county for nine seasons, achieving "the double" of 1,000 runs and 100 wickets in seven of those seasons. He was Wisden Cricketer of the Year in 1955 and awarded his benefit in 1956.

Rawtenstall looked again to Australia in **1952** for their professional and found it in Robert Howard Madden. The right - hand batsman and leg - break bowler sounded like a right hand version of George Tribe. 'Bobby' performed well with the bat scoring 678 runs but his bowling was nowhere near the quality of Tribe with just 22 wickets. Madden was also up against the likes of Weekes (Bacup), Walcott (Enfield), Lindwall (Nelson), Alley (Colne) and Mankad (Haslingden) so it was a tough baptism for the New South Wales man. Two amateurs though led the way in the league statistics, being the leading wicket taker and highest run scorer respectively. The wickets came from Bob Banks who took a career best 70 and the runs from Tommy Incles (772) who had his best ever year with the bat. Wicketkeeper John Jordan had six victims (4 caught and 2 stumped) in the game at East Lancashire and still ended up on the losing side. Fourth place was commendable considering the lack of wickets from the professional.

Controversial President

The league celebrated their jubilee in 1952 and Rawtenstall president, George Whittaker, at the league dinner to celebrate, spoke out strongly about the leagues reluctance and resistance to change. Whittaker was responsible for many innovative developments at Bacup Road including ground development, installation of a public address system and firing rockets over the town on Saturday evenings when Rawtenstall had won. Whittaker though, was at odds with the league committee and they nearly threw the club out of the league as Whittaker said the club would join the Central League. The other Rawtenstall committee members were at odds with Whittaker's decisions and had to placate the league executive. This led to some difficult times for the club until Whittaker ceased to be president.

Australia bound again were the Rawtenstall committee for **1953** securing the services of Alan Keith Walker. Walker was an all-rounder in every sense of the word having also played Rugby Union for his country. A left-arm fast medium bowler and attacking lower order right hand batsman, Walker (left) would go on to appear in 49 first-class matches for Nottinghamshire (1954 -1958). Walker made exactly 500 runs with assistance from Incles, Greenwood and Eric Howarth who all scored 300+. With the ball he took 59 wickets and a best of 7-35 against Nelson at home which they lost. Philip White had the best bowling figures though taking 8-32 at Haslingden in a match which Rawtenstall also lost! The season also saw keeper John Jordan play his final games before heading off to Lancashire. He did though return to the club for a few matches in 1961. Jordan played 62 matches for Lancashire from 1955-1957. Lancashire Captain Cyril Washbrook rated him as one of the best keepers in the country. Had he been a more accomplished batsman, perhaps an England cap could have come his way.

Despite only winning two games the previous year, Walker was invited back for **1954.** There were more victories but batting performances were disappointing. Walker was top scorer with 409 runs. On the bowling front Walker led the way with 59 wickets including 9-42 at Enfield and an all-round display against East Lancashire at home where he took 8-16 and scored his highest innings of 92. Steve Wells (44) enabled more victories but still a bottom half finish was all that could be achieved.

Ground Purchased

The best news possible for supporters of cricket and Rawtenstall arrived in 1955 with the purchase of the ground. It had in fact been presented to the club by the Whittaker family who were landlords of the property. It was donated in memory of the Worswick family and would be known as 'The Worswick Memorial Ground'. Rawtenstall Cricket Club could rest easy knowing that cricket would be not only safe but guaranteed for as long as the game would be played.

After six consecutive years of Australian professionals Rawtenstall ventured back to India for their paid man of 1955. Vijay Hazare was available again and quickly signed up. The man who did the double in 1949 didn't disappoint with 1041 runs including 2 centuries and nine 50s. Philip White (399), including his highest score for the club (90) at home to Ramsbottom and Geoffrey Bradshaw (345) were the other contributors. Hazare (56) and Bob Banks (53) were the leading bowlers in a season which promised so much yet failed to deliver.

Winston Place (below) retired from county cricket in 1955 and the following year he coached at Butlin's Holiday Camp. In 1957 he had a spell umpiring in the County Championship though he was keen to return home. Winston Place never forgot his Rawtenstall roots and he opened a newsagents shop which he ran for the next 21 years. He regularly attended the games offering a quiet snippet of advice for the young and up-and-coming players.

Place was the quieter, more modest partner to the panache of Cyril Washbrook. Of Lancashire's 18 highest opening partnership records, this pair holds three, including the second highest, 350 against Sussex at Old Trafford in 1947. Place's record highlighted below needs no further commentary and if he hadn't had such a wonderful career for Lancashire who knows how many runs he would have scored for his town team.

	M	I	N/O	Runs	H/S	Ave	100	50	Ct
England 1947/48	3	6	1	144	107	28.80	1	0	0
Lancashire 1937/55	324	487	49	15609	266*	35.63	36	71	191
Rawtenstall 1929/56	142	141	19	2493	111*	20.43	2	11	58

24 year old Jayasingh M Ghorpade (right) was considered to be the best all-rounder in India according to Vijay Hazare and would become the club's second Indian professional for **1956**. He just managed to perform the mini double of 500 runs and 50 wickets.

Winston Place's second century happened in 1956 in his last ever appearance in a Lancashire League match against Burnley at Bacup Road. At the age of 42 the worldly wise Place put on 162 for the second wicket with Philip White, chasing down Burnley's score of 180 in just 30 overs. Scholars of a different kind could now make use of the Rossendale College of Further Education which also opened in that year.

It was back to Australia for season **1957** with Victor Edward Jackson recruited. Jackson (below) had played county cricket for Leicestershire for the past 10 years. At Rawtenstall he scored 618 runs and took 72 wickets. Tommy Incles had a good season too with the bat hitting 481 runs including his only century for the club (127 not out at home) chasing down the Todmorden total of 221. The season also saw the first team debut of 18 year old wicketkeeper Brian Manning.

It would be' bridesmaids' again in the Worsley Cup final for the fourth time in what was an embarrassing final against Ramsbottom at Bacup Road.

After a bye in the first round and victories over Colne and Church in the semi-final where Steve Wells hit 55 to steer the side home, they faced Ramsbottom at Bacup Road. The Ramsbottom professional, Fuller, took 7-11 to dismiss Rawtenstall for just 36 runs! The irony being two years later Fuller would become Rawtenstall's professional.

Rawtenstall Worsley Cup Runners Up 1957

Back: P White, S Wells, H Greenwood, EH Howarth, G Holt, V Jackson (pro).

Seated: A Smith, T Incles, R Banks (capt), WB Haughton, K Barnes.

1957 Australian pro Vic Jackson, far right, walks out with the team

Crowd outside the pavilion 1957

Jackson returned for the **1958** season and made 600 runs and took 50 wickets in a year that only saw three defeats. However there were not enough victories either and with 16 drawn games there would never be a title challenge. A fifth place though was encouraging. Incles (630) had his second best season. Geoff Holt (362) was also among the runs but sadly no-one else could provide further backup. Steve Wells with 45 wickets including 5-11 off just 3.2 overs at home to East Lancashire also had his second best season.

Earlier in the year, on 24th May in fact, a stone was unveiled by Robert Worswick to commemorate the gift of the ground to the club by the Whittaker family. The stone still proudly sits amongst the railings on Bacup Road.

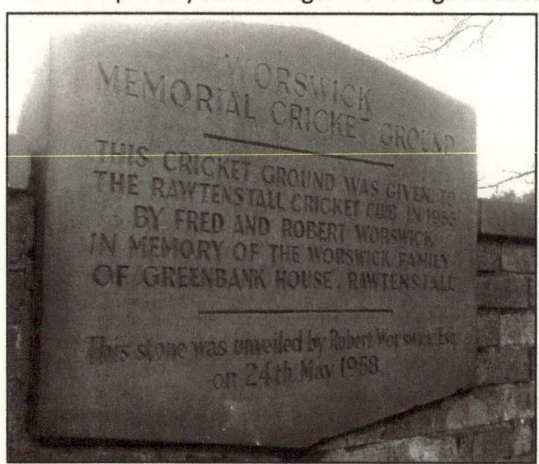

In the Worsley Cup, after victory over Haslingden, who were bowled out for just 48 in the first round, Rawtenstall were on the receiving end of something rather special in the second round when Bacup would be the visitors. The game took place over 6 days in a timeless single innings game.

76

Batting first, Rawtenstall made 302 with professional Jackson making 92 and, batting at no.9, Richard Smith 73. In reply Everton Weekes opened the batting and proceeded to carry his bat through the innings. Bacup were all out for 354 and had won by 52 runs. Weekes was 225 not out. It was the third highest individual innings in the history of the cup.

1959 saw the signing of a South African test player Edward Russell Henry Fuller (right). He played in seven Tests from 1953 to 1957, a right-handed lower-order batsman who made useful runs in domestic South African cricket, and a bowler of right-arm medium-fast cutters. Weather-wise the summer was one of the driest on record since 1947 but it wasn't particularly good for the South African – he mustered only 281 runs although he did take 60 wickets. The leading batsman was Geoff Holt who had his best season by some distance – 538 runs with five 50+ scores. Incles (495) and Ken Barnes (455), including his one and only century, 102 not out at home against Lowerhouse, were the other significant contributors. Three bowlers all took 20+ wickets but it was not enough support for Fuller and the season ended in mid-table. The second eleven though were Junior League Champions for the fifth time. Under the captaincy of Harold Hannah, two players in this squad would go on to become significant first team players in the 1960s and 70s, batsman and future captain Keith French and wicketkeeper Brian Manning.

Rawtenstall v Bacup 1959 - Rawtenstall are fielding

Rawtenstall Junior League Champions 1959

Back: Fred Nicholls, Frank Bridge, Keith French, Geoff Guy, Norman Slater, Jack Wilson.

Front: Jackie Wixted, Harrold Hannah (capt), Brian Manning, Geoff Thomson, Albert Smith.

	Played	W	D	L	Pts	Position
1950	**26**	**12**	**11**	**3**	**47**	**2/14**
1951	26	11	11	4	44	3/14
1952	26	8	14	4	38	4/14
1953	26	2	17	7	23	11/14
1954	26	5	12	9	27	11/14
1955	26	6	10	10	28	10/14
1956	26	5	12	9	32	12/14
1957	26	5	14	7	34	9/14
1958	26	7	16	3	44	5/14
1959	26	8	8	10	40	8/14

Best season of the decade in bold

1960 - 1969 Sunny Afternoon

Following in the footsteps of Vijay Hazare would always be difficult for Rawtenstall's third Indian professional. With a first-class career spanning from 1952-1973, Chandrakant Gulabrao Borde (left) or C.G. Borde as he was more regularly known to many, played in 251 first class matches scoring a stunning 12805 runs and taking 331 wickets. He made his International Test debut for India against West Indies at Mumbai in November 1958 where he went on to score 109 and 96 in his first Test Series. A fearless player of fast bowling, Borde played 55 Tests, scoring 3061 runs, with his highest being 177 not out. He also scored five centuries including two in two Tests. With the ball, Borde took 52 Test wickets with his best being 5/88, as well as 37 catches.

Borde was with Rawtenstall for four consecutive seasons (**1960-63**) and again in 1966. He was a right hand bat and leg break bowler. His first season saw 736 runs with six 50s with good support from Eric Howarth (456) and Ken Barnes (399) and 78 wickets including nine 5 wicket hauls. Bob Banks (48) and Steve Wells (31) also assisted. The away game at Nelson witnessed a tight finish with Rawtenstall only making 96. However Bob Banks took 7-35 to bowl Nelson out for 84.

The lasting league memory though will be Rawtenstall being skittled out at home for just 40 against Bacup. No-one made double figures due to the brutal and frightening pace of Roy Gilchrist (7-24). Lancashire and England sub pro Roy Tattersall played his one and only game for Rawtenstall in this game as, for some reason, Borde was unavailable.

The lasting cup memory had a far better outcome. In the first round tie at home to Ramsbottom on 17th May Bob Banks took an amazing nine wickets including seven clean bowled. Ramsbottom were 78 all out and Banks figures were:

12.1 Overs, 4 Maidens, 21 Runs, 9 Wickets.

It equalled Fred Haworth's league record of 1916 as he became only the second amateur in the clubs history to take nine wickets.

In **1961** Borde made 842 runs including his one century, 111 not out at Bacup in a drawn game that also saw him take 6 wickets. In April the team were dismissed for just 55 at Accrington where a certain West Indian fast bowler by the name of Wes Hall took 8-24. Borde took 7-45 in the away victory over East Lancashire in August which proved to be his best performance of the season. Jack Wilson with 338 and Eric Howarth with 326 runs were the support for Borde whilst Bob Banks (40) and Jeff Guy (35) helped with the ball. Fifth place in the league and the Rawtenstall faithful felt that a challenge for the title was on the cards.

1962 though was to be a disappointing conclusion with a mid-table position. With 602 runs and 72 wickets, Borde had a poor season compared to his previous. Eric Howarth (392) was the other main contributor whilst Banks took 52 wickets where most batsmen in the league were keen to avoid the terror and pace of Roy Gilchrist at Bacup and Wes Hall at Accrington.

1963 saw Borde performances diminish again. This time it was 506 runs and 57 wickets. Youngster Brian Chapman made 355 including his first 50 but few victories and many draws meant a bottom two place although young wicketkeeper Brian Manning also made his first 50 for the club. The bowling accolades went to Banks with 39 scalps including 7-57 at home to Church. In the Cup a first round win over Haslingden saw debutant amateur S Jackson take 5-36 for the Bacup Road men. It was derby time again but defeat in the second round against Bacup.

With the success of the Caribbean quickies across the league Rawtenstall felt they should embrace this idea and signed, in **1964**, West Indian Lester King (opposite). King was a right arm fast bowler from Jamaica and the Rawtenstall committee were hopeful that he could emulate the performances of other quick Caribbean professionals who were dominating the league at that time.

King came with a pedigree; only nine West Indian players have taken a five wicket haul on their test debut and King was one of them. It took place on 13th April 1962 against India at Sabina Park, Jamaica. The 23 year old took 5-46 and ironically one of his wickets was the man who he replaced at Rawtenstall, none other than CG Borde! Surprisingly after this feat, King only played one more test match, although competition as a fast bowler for the West Indies was very intense.

At Rawtenstall King took 58 wickets including 7-51 in a home win over Lowerhouse. However King only managed 343 runs. Leading scorer was Chapman with 374 followed by Manning with 314. Banks with 28 wickets had a poor season by his standards but he was the leading amateur bowler. A tie in the game at Haslingden in May where both sides made 95 was as exciting as it got.

It was another West Indian quickie that was making all the news in the league though. Signed by Burnley in 1964 he took 5 wickets or more in every game with a best of 9-26. In total he took 164 wickets and frightened the living daylights out of most batsmen. At Burnley he took 7-31 to skittle the Bacup Road men all out for 63. At Rawtenstall he took 7-80 on the last game of the season with a spirted 41 coming from opener Rhys Stansfield … His name… if you haven't already guessed was Charles Christopher Griffith.

King was employed by the club again in **1965**. The season started on the same day that the group - The Animals- famous for 'House of the Rising Sun' and many other hits, appeared at The Astoria Ballroom.

Professional Lester King's reputation was rising too as he tore in to take 6-18 in a drawn game at Nelson. King clearly enjoyed playing Nelson as in the return match he scored 100 not out in what was one of only three centuries made by any league player or professional all season, indeed the only amateur to score a ton was Bacup's Barry Wilson.

The sixties saw many famous faces and groups play at The Astoria Ballroom and it was another super group The Who, starring on 22nd May 1965. It was derby day at Bacup Road as Haslingden were the visitors. As The Who were belting out their latest hit "I Can't Explain" there were a few sorry faces amongst the Rawtenstall eleven who, after being bowled out for 109, were trying to explain a 45 run defeat to the Rawtenstall faithful. There was also another tied game at Todmorden where each side scored just 61 runs.

Whilst King had been a reasonable success (470 runs and 70 wickets) the results said otherwise with too many drawn games. Brian Chapman (351) and Maurice Davies (38 wickets) were the leading amateurs.

Rawtenstall said goodbye to King as indeed in 1965 cotton was no longer king in the valley as the footwear industry was now the largest employer in the town with over 3000 employees closely followed by 2500 in cotton and weaving and 1500 in the felt and textile finishing fields.

More superstars were hitting the Astoria stage with The Walker Brothers the latest sensation to pack them in. Making their second appearance on 19th June **1966** they were mobbed by gangs of young women eager to meet their heartthrobs. The Rawtenstall committee "made it easy on themselves" by re-signing Chandu Borde for his final season with the club.

The other ball game was hitting the headlines in 1966 as the World Cup fever was in town and capturing the thrills of many who were glued to their black and white televisions. It must have been a distraction for the players as well – particularly Borde who only took 18 wickets – Rod Taylor (35) was top of the list. Borde did score 736 runs supported by D Cannon (388), Brian Chapman (338) and Brian Manning (311) however only Bacup and Ramsbottom would finish below them.

Chandu Borde leads out his team mates for his last game in 1966.

What Rawtenstall needed was a bowler who could bowl teams out.

Well credit to the Rawtenstall committee because they found it in the short and strongly built 26 year old Australian John William Grant. Grant (left and below) was a bustling opening bowler and hard-hitting lower-order batsman who played 43 matches for Victoria State in five seasons.

He had three very productive years as professional for Rawtenstall helping them achieve runners up spot in **1967** and **1968**. In 1967 he took 95 wickets at an average of 8.41 and made 275 runs at 17.26. No batsman scored over 300 runs – Geoff Heaton (298) being the highest run getter. However Grant's wickets included 5 wickets or more in eleven games including a best of 8-31 at home to Ramsbottom. Rod Taylor was the perfect foil at the other end and 6-19 at home to Church would contribute to his 29 wickets for the season. Winning nine games would give them a well-deserved second spot.

Grant had an excellent season the following year. He took a very impressive 125 wickets at 9.98 and made 506 runs at 28.23. The amateur batting was also backing the Aussie up with Heaton (610), Chapman (409) and Keith French (338) the contributors.

1968 also saw the debut of a young 17 year old batsman by the name of Peter George Wood who would go on to break all the Rawtenstall and Lancashire League batting records over the next 28 years. More of him in the next 3 decades! It also saw the final season of stalwart Philip White who had served the club well for 30 years.

Rawtenstall League Runners Up 1967

Back: F Lord, D Ramsbottom, R Taylor, BR Stansfield, K French, G Heaton.

Seated, G Lord, B Manning, P White (capt), J Grant (pro), B Chapman.

It was the bowling performances from Grant that enabled Rawtenstall to repeat their runners up achievement from the previous year. With fourteen 5 - wicket matches or more, Grant clearly had a liking for the Rawtenstall wickets as 9-29 v Accrington, 8-29 v Nelson, 8-57 v Rishton, 7-15 v Church and 7-66 v Haslingden were his star turns, all at Bacup Road. The figures for the Accrington game were the best by any Rawtenstall bowler in modern cricket - you have to go back to Ed Smith in 1925 to find similar league figures. In a remarkable drawn game at Burnley he had the figures of:
15 overs, 8 maidens, 9 runs, 7 wickets.

Strike partner Rod Taylor had his best season with 44 wickets, including 6-18 at home to Burnley. This time it was 13 wins behind Champions Enfield.

Grant was unavailable for **1969** so 'tall and brooding', as described by Wisden, Aussie Dave Renneberg was employed. Selected for the Australian 1966-67 tour of South Africa, he made his debut partnering Graham McKenzie in the first Test at Johannesburg and went on to play in all five Tests.

He kept his place in the home series against India the following winter, but was dropped after the third Test of the four-match series. He toured England in 1968 without playing in any of the Tests, taking 41 wickets including a career-best 8 for 71 against Essex. With that grounded pedigree it was felt that Rawtenstall had someone who could do the damage similar to Grant. How wrong they were Renneberg (left) scored just 253 runs with a top score of 37 not out. With the ball he fared better although for an opening test fast bowler 63 wickets would never win over many plaudits.

It was however another bowler who did - George Croisdale, who took 52 wickets including 7-16 at home against Lowerhouse. However with just one win all season the Bacup Road supporters couldn't wait to get John Grant back for 1970.

Elsewhere in the valley there were some outlandish ideas being considered for an outdoor ski slope in the town – well there were plenty of hills that could accommodate one – but skiing in Rawtenstall ...really?!

	P	W	D	L	Pts	Position	Note
1960	26	9	7	10	44	8/14	inc 2 pts for tie
1961	26	10	11	5	51	5/14	
1962	26	7	10	9	38	8/14	
1963	26	3	15	8	27	13/14	
1964	26	4	13	9	30	11/14	inc 2 pts for tie
1965	26	4	18	4	35	9/14	inc 2 pts for tie
1966	26	4	13	9	29	12/14	
1967	**26**	**9**	**14**	**3**	**50**	**2/14**	
1968	**26**	**13**	**10**	**3**	**68**	**2/14**	**Inc 6 bonus pts**
1969	26	1	12	13	23	13/14	Inc 6 bonus pts

Best seasons of the decade in bold

1970 - 1979 Aint no stopping us now

After the disappointment of 1969, John Grant returned in **1970** for a season that many hoped would see the club go one better than the runners up spot they had achieved with Grant back in 1967 and 1968. It wasn't quite to be and in a very close finish Burnley were champions with 61 points, Enfield runners up with 60 points and Rawtenstall third with 58 points.

Brian Chapman scored his one and only century for the club in 1970. It came in the last game of the season at Bacup Road against Lowerhouse. Rawtenstall declared on 179-2 and skittled Lowerhouse out for 69 with John C Davies taking 6-28. Chapman was leading scorer with 693 runs followed by professional Grant (583) and Heaton (484). Grant took 89 wickets including 9-36 at home to Church, whilst spinner Davies took 36 wickets.

Australian, Terrence James Jenner (1944 -2011) played nine Tests from 1970 to 1975 and he was signed as professional in **1971.** Primarily a leg-spin bowler he was known for his attacking, loopy style of bowling, but he was also a handy lower-order batsman. In his later years he was a leg-spin coach to many players around the world and a great influence on a future Lancashire League professional and test star Shane Warne.

The league introduced limited overs for the first time in an attempt to bring more exciting cricket to the league and reduce the number of drawn games. Jenner (below) managed 480 runs and a top score of 68 not out. Good support came from Geoff Heaton (379), Brian Chapman (355) and, in his first full season with the club, 21 year old Peter Wood (338). Jenner took 65 wickets including 7-33 at home against Colne but the bowling plaudits went to George Croisdale with 52 scalps. Wicketkeeper Brian Manning had his best season behind the stumps with 33 victims (21 caught and 12 stumped) . The year also saw the first of three junior league championships.

South African David Lynton Orchard was recruited for the next two seasons. His fame would come later on in life as an international umpire who stood in 44 Tests and 107 One-Day Internationals.

Rawtenstall Junior League Champions 1971

Back: W Davies, RS Benn, F Lord, G Nuttall, K French, P Wood, ME Davies.

Front: BR Stansfield, TG Holt, K Barnes (capt), B Payne, A Robinson.

The first season (**1972**) was a success with Orchard (below) scoring 619 runs and taking 57 wickets. Support came from Chapman (387) with the bat and Croisdale (54) with the ball. In the Worsley Cup there was a close first round win at home agaist Accrington. Rawtenstall made 146-8 in their 36 x 8 ball overs with Duncan Ramsbottom batting at no.7, making an invaluable 59 not out. Accrington's reply fell 4 runs short with Orchard and Croisdale each taking five wickets. It was another tight win over Nelson in the second round by just 9 runs – Croisdale again taking five scalps. The semi-final tie at home to East Lancashire went the way of the Blackburn men, however third place in the league and a semi-final place in the cup and everyone was on a high.

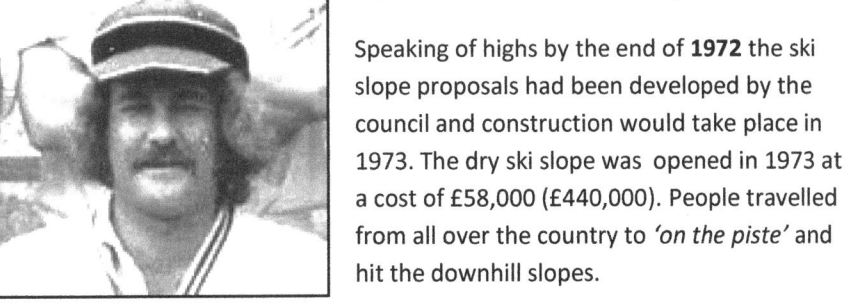

Speaking of highs by the end of **1972** the ski slope proposals had been developed by the council and construction would take place in 1973. The dry ski slope was opened in 1973 at a cost of £58,000 (£440,000). People travelled from all over the country to *'on the piste'* and hit the downhill slopes.

At Bacup Road it was a downhill year as well. Too many defeats left Rawtenstall with their lowest league position of the decade just above wooden spoonists Colne. Having said that there were some excellent individual performances. Orchard (623), Chapman (614) and Wood (458) all scored well. Chapman made his second century and highest score 125 v Haslingden at home in an opening partnership with Keith French of 149 in a match that was won by the visitors. Despite the runs there were only four victories all season.

1974 saw the re-organisation of local government. Rossendale Borough Council was formed taking the towns of Rawtenstall, Bacup and Haslingden to form an administration that many today feel and wish should never have taken place.

Rawtenstall elected to venture back to the Carribean for their second West Indian professional John Wakefield Holder (below) in an attempt to improve on the previous year. The 29 year old Barbadian had played county cricket for Hampshire 1968-72. He was also professional for other clubs within the Lancashire leagues between 1974 and 1982 including Milnrow, Norden and Royton although his first year was at Rawtenstall. Two amateur batsmen scored over 600 runs. Firstly Peter Wood (657) includng five 50s followed closely by the captain Keith French (617) including his only century, 102 not out in a drawn game at home to Lowerhouse. It was a good job that the two amateurs scored well as Holder only managed 181 runs. Though the bowling was disappointing with Holder leading the way with just 34 scalps, it was an improvement of the previous year's league position.

1975 saw the Bacup Road Picture House close as a single screen venue and re-open with 4 screens seating 121, 118, 165 and 118 and creatively re-named 'Unit Four Cinema'. One film released in April of that year was "Monty Python and the Holy Grail". However you couldn't see it in Rawtenstall as the council (one of 39 across the country) banned it from being shown in the Borough for blasphemy – they wouldn't even give it an X rated certificate!

Rawtenstall employed South African David John Brickett in an attempt to turn around their fortunes and provide some decent spiritual entertainment. The man from Port Elizabeth made a gallant effort scoring 913 runs with a top score of 92 not out. The amateurs were also scoring well with Chapman (517), French (505), and Payne (427) all contributing well. George Croisdale led the way with the ball taking 62 wickets including 7-36 at Nelson. He was ably supported by the professional with 49 scalps. Despite these positive contributions a mid-table finish was all that could be achieved.

There was an exceptional all-round performance though from George Croisdale. It happened in the first round of the Worsley Cup at home against Lowerhouse on 1st June. Lowerhouse batted first and scored an impressive 240 - 9 in their 36 eight ball overs. Croisdale took 5-78 off 16 overs and maybe thought his work was done. However when Rawtenstall batted Croisdale came in at a promoted no.5 spot and proceeded to smash 109 not out to see Rawtenstall to victory in less than 29 overs. It was an impressive display by the fast bowler whose previous high score in cup games had been 12! It would be defeat to Burnley in the second round, but a cup run wasn't far away. The 2nd eleven had success winning the championship as another young batsman was making his debut for the first eleven. Little did the Rawtenstall public know that over the next 25 years he would go on to become the second highest run scorer in the clubs history, scoring over 10,000 league runs. His name was Glenn Barlow.

Rawtenstall Junior League Champions 1975

Back: F Tattersall, JC Davies, JG Cook, B Howarth, A Hindle, B Davies, B Terry, A Hanson.

Front : P Riding (scorer) TG Holt, D Wood, BR Stansfield (capt), J Seal, P Barnes.

1976 The Double

Ninety years since the club's formation and continuous play at Bacup Road, the long hot summer of 1976 saw many a record broken but for Rawtenstall it would re-write their history as they won the league and cup double for the first time.

After winning the Worsley Cup in one of the best ever finals, Rawtenstall became the first club to complete the double since East Lancashire 10 years previously. They were crowned Champions for the first time in 50 years after a terrific title race that saw the club gradually climb to the summit with just one match to go after a spectacular loss of form by long time leaders East Lancashire.

After 11 matches East Lancashire were 7 points clear at the top of the league with 20 points more than Rawtenstall. They were top from May 15th until August 29th but won only 5 of their last 15 matches. Rawtenstall had a terrible start and after 6 matches had only won two games but then won 12 of their last 14 matches to win the title right at the death.

It was a season of tremendous cricket played on long hot summer days after some of the early matches had been rained off. The crowds flocked back as the sun shone with every match now producing a positive result. Gate receipts exceeded £10,000 (£76,000) for the first time.

Haslingden professional Peter Swart was the outstanding player of the season almost achieving the coveted double by scoring 1022 runs and taking 94 wickets. However Rawtenstall had Syed Abid Ali (right) taking 82 wickets and also hitting 422 runs, supported by Peter Wood (732), Keith French (462) and George Croisdale (41 wickets).

Ali was that rare combination of Hyderabadi flair and the exuberance of youth: in an era when fielding and running-between-the-wickets were alien concepts, Abid was different in a refreshing fashion. He was dynamic, athletic, energetic, and a sheer delight to watch. He fielded like no one did in his era. He ran extremely fast, had the fitness of a gymnast, never gave up, and maintained the same energy level throughout the day. The same applied when he ran between the wickets his sheer presence converted the 1s into 2s and 2s into 3s.

A few years later some of the players recalled the final and Abid Ali. Wicketkeeper Brian Manning on Ali:

> "Abid Ali was an incredible player in so many different respects. It was principally his bowling which helped us. He got just over 400 runs with the bat which was rather modest in comparison with many other professionals but when you turn to his bowling, he bowled 373 overs, 74 maidens, 82 wickets at an average of 13. He kept it tight all season which was critical too. We agreed that I could stand up to him even though at first he was quite reluctant to let me do that because he classed himself as a medium fast bowler, but he used to bowl very good leg and off cutters and that gave us an opportunity for some stumping's over the course of the season. It was also much more challenging for me to stand up which I always loved to do if I could, rather than stand back. This also put more pressure on the batsmen.
>
> We hoped for some success in 1976 because we knew that Abid Ali was an all-round performer. Although his runs weren't that significant the rest of the team played round him. With Peter Wood, Keith French, Terry Holt and Brian Chapman in the front line making sure we made some decent scores from time to time. As the tension built up during the course of the season, there was just a possibility that the double might be on. Abid Ali had appeared with India in the first World Cup in 1975. He was very conscious of his own position as professional and very proud of that as many Indian players have been over the years. He was proud of his position as a Test cricketer even though at Test level his performances had been reasonable but not outstanding as a league pro he was very good for us. People talk about team spirit but team spirit is only engendered when you are winning, the more you win the more the team comes together.

The Worsley Cup Final threw up an unlikely hero in unknown left arm spinner Chris Flood. The 22 year old turned in a match winning performance to provoke headlines such as 'Flood turns the tide', 'Flood swamps Accrington' and 'Come the Flood'. Chris Flood recalls the final:

> "It was overwhelming really. I remember going onto the ground at the beginning and being very nervous because there was a big crowd on. Abid took me out on the field and spent a lot of time with me warming up, bowling to me. He had played in that sort of arena, so he was trying to settle everybody down. When I came on to bowl, I was the last throw of the

dice. I am always nervous when I play and what makes it worse is having to wait around. Accrington kept going and going and nobody was getting wickets so eventually it was: 'Come on Chris have a look.' I knew straight away that the wicket was taking spin. It was overcast so the ball was drifting very nicely for the arm ball. I was really trying to will myself up but I just couldn't get my length right early on, but eventually Peter West had a big flash at me and he hit it straight it to George Croisdale on the cover boundary. This seemed to lift us a bit. We had a foot in the door. When I got Tony Gallagher for my fifth wicket, they set off round the ground with the collection boxes, but then I got Birtwistle and Neville in the same over, the lads were saying 'What are you playing at, we'd barely got halfway down the ground and you've bowled then all out! I got £177 (£1,350) but they said I could have had twice as much if I had let them bat a bit longer. I was elated and wanted to go and hug somebody, but I was aware that the crowd was running on, I was thinking 'I've seen this on telly and you get really mobbed and made a mess of so I thought 'Right I'm off.'

"Abid Ali took me under his wing. To play with him in the team, you just knew he could tie one end down more or less every game. From a bowling point of view, it was a case of what you could do at the other end. George Croisdale would come on and bowl the spit and snarl stuff or the big fat sweaters as I used to call them. After that, many a day I wouldn't get a bowl because George and Abid would do the damage. We had Rod Taylor, who was a fantastic bowler, waiting in the wings not being able to get a game. Graham Cook was also in the team, so I could go many games without getting a bowl.

"For me personally on a coaching level, Abid spent a lot of time with me. He would come and say, 'Bishen (Bedi) would do this or Bishen would do that'. He taught me an awful lot such as how to move about on the crease, how to make the same ball a different length, not that I could particularly do it, but that was the theory behind it! He taught me an awful lot that he had picked up from Bishen Bedi".

Rawtenstall captain Keith French on the final:

"At the interval we talked about our performance and although it was not a great score for Accrington to chase (137) we thought that if we bowled and fielded well we would make it quite difficult for them. Accrington too got off to a very good start despite the fact that we were bowling and fielding well. Something had to happen for us – it did in the form of a young left arm spinner by the name of Chris Flood. I brought him on at the pavilion end and he turned on quite a performance taking seven Accrington wickets for 40 runs. He was just sensational. With some very fine fielding and a brilliant piece of stumping by the 'BAM' (**B**rian **A**ndrew **M**anning)to get rid of Ian Birtwistle who was causing us a little concern for his 'stickability' at no.8. Abid was tying up the Kay Street end, which forced Accrington to chance their arm against 'Floodie'...they failed. The pitch invasion at the end of the game was amazing...people (players and spectators alike) hugging everybody and anybody. Floodie was the 'Hero' of the game and totally mobbed. The like of which had not been witnessed before or since. WHAT A DAY!!!"

Gate receipts (40p entry) for the day were £1,451 (£11,000)

George Croisdale receives the Evening Telegraph Tankard for the fastest 50.

Other players are (left to right) K French, G Lord, G Cook, P Wood, B Manning, G Croisdale, T Holt, C Flood.

The **1977** season also saw temperatures soar again nearly matching those of the previous year. However on the field it was a case of "after the Lord Mayor's show" as Rawtenstall were never close to repeating the exploits of 76.

Abid Ali was again the paid man and Rawtenstall had recruited a young 20 year old amateur left handed opening batsman from Accrington. He only lasted one season before Lancashire and eventually England called upon him but for that one season and in just 18 innings he hit 600 runs including a century (128) at home against Todmorden. In that short period of time the Rawtenstall members knew they were watching a talent that could take any bowling apart. The young man in question was Graeme Fowler. In September, Fowler and Peter Wood put together a partnership of 149 in just 72 minutes in a total of 254 for 2 at home against Todmorden.

Spiritually it was a good year for Abid Ali to go to Church, as he scored 103 there in an opening partnership of 174 with Fowler (70) which was the best opening partnership since the war. Ali then took 7-49 to enable Rawtenstall to take the four points. Peter Wood hit 494 runs for the season including 100 at home to Church. Ali notched 620 runs and 78 wickets. In some ways, a better performance than the double year but too many defeats meant a mid-table place was all that could be achieved.

In the cup, after a first round bye, it was defeat at home to eventual runners up Enfield. Ali took 6-57 but it was Ali's Indian compatriot Maden Lal who did the damage for Enfield taking 6-43.

Back: D Flood (Scorer), BW Chapman, S Abid Ali (pro), PG Wood, G Croisdale, WG Lord, JC Cook, R Medlock (manager)

Seated: BA Manning, B Payne, K French (capt), TG Holt, C Flood.

Rawtenstall Double winning Team 1976

In **1978** Ali had an amazing year with the bat scoring 922 runs including a century (106) against Accrington at home where he also took 6-64. He notched nine 50+ scores. But it was also a case of "anything you can do Ali – I can pretty much match" as amateur Peter Wood hit 912 runs including 103 at home to Church and eight 50+ scores. It wasn't the end of the centurions either as Glenn Barlow scored the highest of the lot (108 not out) and his first century for the club at home to Colne. Payne (441) and Barlow (378) provided further ammunition with the bat.

Ali took 76 wickets but the only other support forthcoming was from up and coming young 17 year old fast bowler Brett Storey who took 25 wickets in his first full season. Despite all the runs too many games were lost and another mid-table position would be attained. One exciting finish was a tied game at Burnley each team scoring 148.

There was though one particular game at Bacup Road that is etched in the minds of those who attended. It took place on 18th June against East Lancashire in the second round of the Worsley Cup. East Lancashire had a 23 year old left handed Australian batsman as professional in their ranks who produced one of the finest innings ever witnessed. Batting first, East Lancs scored 290-4 in their allotted 36 x 8 ball overs. The Aussie took the Rawtenstall bowling apart finishing on 179 not out ... his name? Allan Border. Ali went for 121 runs in his 16 overs. Could Rawtenstall get anywhere near this score? Losing Barlow and Payne at 49-2 it looked unlikely but then Peter Wood and Abid Ali did exactly what Border had done. Wood eventually went for 83 and Brian Manning joined his professional. The hard hitting continued and with 1 over left Ali (119 not out) and Manning (58 not out) saw Rawtenstall home in a truly memorable victory.

In the semi-final at home to Todmorden 87 from opener Barlow ensured another final would be reached at home again this time to Enfield. In a tight game Enfield won by just 7 runs.

Abid Ali departed after three wonderful seasons which would be held in the memories of not only Rawtenstall followers but many Lancashire League fans.

Year	Runs	Highest	Ave	Wickets	Best	Ave
1976	427	54	22	**82**	7-46	**13**
1977	620	103	33	78	**7-44**	15
1978	**922**	**106**	**44**	76	6-33	17

Abid Ali League record for Rawtenstall

Rawtenstall Worsley Cup Runners Up 1978

Back: A Hanson, B Terry, J Beaumont, G Barlow, B Storey, A Nuttall, N Chadwick, G Horrocks.

Seated: W Lord, P Riding, B Manning, P Wood (capt), B Payne, S Abid Ali (pro).

Where would Rawtenstall turn to in **1979** in an attempt to fill Ali's boots? India, Australia, Africa or the West Indies? Well they travelled as far as Accrington in their search and found it in 36 year old Alan Worsick (below) who had a prolific career as an amateur for his home town club and played just one game for Lancashire in 1978.

The Rawtenstall committee clearly felt that they had the amateur batting talent to deal with any attack in the league. What was needed was a bowler who could win games rather than contain. They were nearly right insofar as more games were won and the amateur batsmen performed well again. This time Barlow led the way with 630 and his second century (101 not out) at home to Enfield. Not far behind was Payne with 599, followed by Wood (489). Worsick took 54 wickets including the best league bowling figures of the season, 8-29 at home against Ramsbottom. Worsick was ably supported by John Beaumont (35); including 6-17 against his old club Bacup at Lanehead. Fourth place was a good way to end the decade.

There have been some tight finishes for Rawtenstall in Worsley Cup games over the years but none tighter than on 24th June. It was a second round tie at Haslingden who had just made 111 all out of 34 overs with Worsick taking 6-32. Rawtenstall looked to be coasting at 103-6 but a mini-collapse started and the overs were running out. Following two run-outs, last pair John Beaumont and Paul Riding were at the crease and scrambled a run of the last ball. The scores were level... it was a tie....But Rawtenstall won by losing fewer wickets. The second eleven also finished the year on a high with their third championship in 10 years.

Rawtenstall Junior League Champions 1979

Back: S Lord (scorer), WG Lord, A Nuttall, JG Cook, BW Chapman, R Ashworth, A Hindle, TJ Hussey, S Pickles.

Front: S Tattersall, R Holmes, AF Robinson (capt), D Watson, P Barnes.

	P	W	D	L	Pts	Position	Note
1970	26	12	10	4	58	3/14	
1971	26	10	12	4	51	8/14	11 bonus pts
1972	26	13	7	6	60	3/14	8 b pts
1973	26	4	12	10	28	13/14	
1974	26	4	17	5	33	9/14	
1975	26	13	1	12	61	7/14	9 b point
1976	**26**	**17**	**3**	**7**	**75**	**1/14**	**7 b point**
1977	26	12	4	10	54	9/14	6 b point
*1978	26	12	3	10	55	7/14	5 b point
1979	26	14	4	8	66	4/14	6 b point

Best season of the decade in bold. * includes 1 tied result

1980 - 1989 Just can't get enough

The decade started with the recruitment of Graeme Thomson Ross (left) an Australian from Victoria State. Ross had a reasonable season with 507 runs and 65 wickets including 8-57 at home against Ramsbottom. The amateurs were on fine form Peter Wood led from the front with the bat hitting 917 runs including a century and eight 50s. Offering strong support were Payne (554) and Barlow (482). Bowling-wise Alan Worswick (now playing as an amateur) took 43 wickets and off spinner Roger Watson (32). Third place in the league and many were thinking, with this squad, anything was possible especially if a strike bowler could be found. The clubs 2nd team also won the Championship repeating their success of the previous year. Rawtenstall train station finally closed in 1980 when a regular coal train was withdrawn by British Rail.

The express strike bowler came in the form of the club's third West Indian professional Franklyn DaCosta Stephenson for **1981**. Stephenson (right) was a hard-hitting middle-order batsman and a right-arm fast bowler. In addition he developed a pioneering slower ball and was the first bowler to use it regularly in one-day cricket. A true all-rounder, he first came to prominence playing for the West Indies Young Cricketers team that toured England in 1978.

Stephenson was an instant success both on and off the field. 576 runs was nothing spectacular but with Wood (687), Swanney (490) and Barlow (437) all significant contributors Stephenson's runs were a bonus. Swanney also scored his only century for the club and the highest score in the league all season – 118 not out at home to East Lancashire. It was the bowling of Stephenson that made the difference though – 105 wickets including 11 five + wicket games. He was well supported with Roger Watson's off spin (39). Losing just five games throughout the season, Stephenson had out performed two other West Indian quickies that were also playing in the league. Rishton had Michael Holding and Haslingden Andy Roberts. Other star professionals that season were Indian test greats Kapil Dev, Maden Lal and Mohinder Armanarth. Pakistan was represented by test opener Mohsin Khan and Aftab Baloch. Oh what a treat it was to see such legends of the game play.

Rawtenstall League Champions 1981

P Rush, P Pickles, S Ashworth, G Barlow, B Payne, B Storey, J Swanney, T Farnworth, B Terry, G Lord, F Stephenson with daughter Amanda.

Back: AC Lawrey, S Ashworth, A Hanson, R Watson, B Storey, FD Stephenson (pro) J Beaumont, A Nuttall, G Horrocks, M Ashton (scorer)

Seated: J Swanney, BA Manning, PG Wood (capt), B Payne, G Barlow.

Rawtenstall League Champions 1981

Stephenson returned for **1982** and had competition from his Barbadian compatriots Collis King and Rod Estwick playing respectively for Colne and Todmorden. Rawtenstall were without Peter Wood, but it was pretty much same again this time losing six games and pipping Lowerhouse to the title by just one point.

The batting accolades went to amateurs: Swanney (666), Payne (594) and Stephen Ashworth (466) in his best season for the club, including his only century, 107 not out, in the home victory over Colne. Stephenson also contributed 519 runs and with 99 league wickets. Stephenson again led the way with the ball, this time supported by 21 year old fast bowler Brett Storey who took 40 wickets. Never before had the club achieved back to back title wins – the decade would be the clubs most successful in its history.

'Aggers'

There was even the opportunity for future radio cricket commentator and former Leicestershire County player Johnathan Agnew to experience the joy of Lancashire League cricket. He played just one game as a sub professional in 1982 for Rishton at Haslingden and his performance was not one for the record books. He scored 6 runs and took 3 wickets for 83 runs. Just for information, Haslingden won.

Stephenson joined the rebel West Indies XI, led by Lawrence Rowe and Alvin Kallicharran, that toured South Africa, and played in so-called "Test" matches and "One Day Internationals" against the South African national cricket team that had been barred from world cricket because of apartheid.

The rebel West Indian cricketers were themselves then barred from all levels of West Indies cricket for life, until the ban was lifted in 1989 and Stephenson never played true Test cricket. He is widely regarded as the greatest cricketer never to have played for the West Indies. He moved into county cricket and his first season for Nottinghamshire in 1988 was sensational. Since the reduction in English first-class games in 1969, only one player, the New Zealander Richard Hadlee, had achieved the all-rounder's "double" of 1,000 runs and 100 wickets. Stephenson in 1988 became the second to achieve this feat, making 1018 runs and taking 125 wickets. He was Wisden Cricketer of the Year in 1989 for this achievement and was also the Cricket Society's leading all-rounder.

Without the services of Stephenson, Rawtenstall decided to go a little bit off key with tradition and signed their first ever Zimbabwean professional.

Back: P Ashworth, A Hanson, P Rush, B Storey, FD Stephenson (pro), A Farnworth, G Barlow, M Ashton (scorer)

Seated: R Holmes, S Ashworth, B Payne, (capt) J Swanney, B Terry

Rawtenstall League Champions 1982

The man chosen to succeed Stephenson for the **1983** season was 23 year old Kevin Curran (right) a Zimbabwean all-rounder. It would be a very hard task to emulate the performances of the Bajan. Indeed Curran scored just 438 runs and took 56 wickets. The amateur batsmen were still performing well with Swanney (618), Barlow (511), Ashworth (347) and Payne (316) the key contributors. It was the bowling and the depth of bowling that meant the team would finish in the bottom half of the league. Brett Story with 43 wickets was the exception, but no-one else took more than 15 wickets.

Curran did have one particular stand out game though in the Worsley Cup first round game at Haslingden. In a score of 234-4 Curran scored 118 and then took 6-65 to restrict Haslingden to 171-9.

The club returned to the West Indies in **1984** – in fact South America to be precise, signing Guyana batsman Kamal Singh (below). For the past two seasons Singh had been professional for Rishton scoring 750+ runs and taking 70+ wickets each season. If he could reproduce that sort of form for Rawtenstall then a top six place could well be achieved. Well... Singh did just that... He scored 779 runs and took 60 wickets and Rawtenstall finished sixth. Glenn Barlow had his best ever season by some way scoring 890 runs including two centuries. The first -107 not out at home to Lowerhouse in May but the second one was a bit special.

Rawtenstall were at home to Church on 2nd September and they batted first making 191-9 in 34 x 8 ball overs. Professional Singh took 7-74 – his best bowling performance. Opening the batting for Rawtenstall were Glenn Barlow and Phillip Pickles who proceeded to take apart the Church bowling with aggression and style. Barlow was particularly belligerent on Church stalwarts Jack Holdsworth and Nick Westwell. After 29.1 overs the game was over. Pickles had scored 65 not out but Barlow had hit 126. The 193 run partnership had just beaten the first wicket partnership set way back in 1915 by Leach and Waller by two runs.

Peter Wood with 594 runs, John Swanney with 415 and Stephen Ashworth with 324 ensured it was a run feast that year. Brett Storey with 32 wickets supported Singh but that was it. More wicket takers and more variety was needed if the club were to emulate the success of 81 and 82.

Up the valley at Bacup their young left arm spinner Keith Roscoe was having a few relationship troubles with some members of the Bacup committee. Following the loss of some key players, including Bacup's captain Roger Law, the Bacup professional at the time, New Zealander Ross Ormiston, suggested that Roscoe (left) should try pastures new if he wanted to improve. So for the **1985** season Roscoe left Bacup and became a Rawtenstall player.

The 100 year anniversary of cricket was taking place at Bacup Road and was one to remember in so many ways. Firstly it would be the clubs second win of the Worsley Cup ... or the Lancashire Evening Telegraph Cup as it was known. Secondly the outstanding bowling of Tyrone Anthony "Tony" Merrick from Antigua who was employed for seasons 1985 and 1986.

It was Merrick (right) who was instrumental in the winning of the cup. In a tight first round match at home to Colne, Rawtenstall won by just 16 runs. Batting first Rawtenstall were struggling at 81-5 before Merrick hit 62 in a total of 184. Colne at 136-5 looked to be in control but Rawtenstall found an unlikely bowling hero in Neil Chadwick who took three quick wickets and Colne were all out for 170.

In the second round at East Lancashire Merrick performed again – this time with the ball taking 7-61 in 24 overs, five of which were clean bowled, to restrict the home side to 181. The amateur batsmen were in fine form, Barlow (72) and Pickles (50) put on 111

for the first wicket. Peter Wood and Jonathon Benn each made a brisk 20 and the game was over.

The semi-final was at Turf Moor against Burnley who batted first with test star and popular Pakistani professional Mudassar Nazar opening the batting. However they could only score 124 all out with Merrick taking four wickets and Roscoe three. Openers Barlow and Pickles were again in excellent form hitting 56 and 43 respectively - Rawtenstall won with just two wickets down.

The final would be against Todmorden and it took place at Bacup Road on 7th September. It wasn't the greatest day weather- wise and the competition was reduced from its 48 overs to a 42 over game. Rawtenstall batted first and scored 187-8 with contributions from Swanney (49), Mark Griffin (39) and Merrick (30). Todmorden started well and were 100-4 and looked in control. However it was that man Merrick who again ripped through the batting finishing with 5-61 of 20 overs.

Nine years after the first Worsley Cup win Rawtenstall now had its second.

In the league Wood (707), Pickles (641) and Barlow (544) performed again as did Roscoe (44) and Merrick (86). Sixth place as the title went up the road to Haslingden.

Rawtenstall Worsley Cup Winners 1985

Back: R Singleton (scorer) M Griffin, A Merrick (pro) P Pickles, G Barlow, K Roscoe, J Beaumont, P Ashworth.

Seated: J Swanney, B Payne, PG Wood (Capt), BA Manning, N Chadwick.

Rawtenstall Worsley Cup Winners (Lancashire Evening Telegraph Cup) 1985

1985 Worsley Cup celebrations

1986 saw the retirement of long-serving wicketkeeper Brian Manning. After 29 years dedication his final season was also one of his best - 30 victims (18 caught and 12 stumped were his best figures since 1971). Manning's career brought a total of 471 League victims and 48 in the Worsley cup.

Brian Manning Lancashire League Career Batting and Fielding (1957-1986)

M	I	NO	Runs	HS	Ave	100	50	Ct	St
518	405	75	4148	81*	12.56	0	6	400	71

There were some fine batting performances throughout the year. The depth and quality in the Rawtenstall batting saw seven amateurs all scoring half centuries: Wood, Barlow, Pickles, Kershaw, Griffin, Payne and Benn. Benn turned his fifty into a century, his only one for the club and the only one of the season. It took place at Ramsbottom where Benn opened the innings and carried his bat through to make 111 not out in a total of 222. Ramsbottom posted 183-5 and won the game on run rate. Merrick (72) and Roscoe (51) took the wickets. Wood (768), Barlow (505), Merrick (502), Pickles (432), Kershaw (394) and Griffin (367) all scored well but despite all these excellent performances and winning nine games the club finished second from the bottom.

"Bumble" bumbles Rawtenstall out of cup final place

In the cup it was nearly a repeat of the previous season. A first round win at Church saw Merrick take 7-33. In the second round Rawtenstall faced Haslingden at their Bent Gate ground. Batting first Barlow scored 93 in Rawtenstall's total of 221-9. Merrick though was at it again taking 6-37 to bowl Haslingden out for 127. The semi-final was at home against Accrington. In the Accrington side was future

Lancashire star Graham Lloyd however his father David, aged 39, was also helping his home town club. The former Lancashire and England opener and Sky Sports pundit showed all his class and ability batting at no.6 making 59 not out in Accrington's total of 218-8. Merrick took 5-56 but it was another medium quick bowler, the Accrington professional Rod Tucker, who ripped through the Rawtenstall top order taking 6-31. "Bumble" even chipped in with three wickets and Rawtenstall were 83 all out. Lloyd helped his club win the cup that season before returning to his punditry. Merrick though, was rightly attracting the interests of the Counties and eventually signed for Warwickshire.

The Unit 4 Picture House would close again in 1986, although it re-opened under another owner who operated just one screen seating 120 but with video recorders and DVD technology on the increase, the writing was on the wall for a small screen cinema.

The **1987** season saw a true international cricket star grace the Lancashire League. Rishton signed none other than Isaac Vivian Alexander Richards – Viv to you and me! Richards availability was made possible by the acrimonious crisis that had engulfed Somerset CCC the previous year, when the decision was made mid-season to release the club's two long-serving West Indian greats, Richards and Joel Garner, which prompted the departure of Ian Botham in solidarity. Richards hadn't sought another first-class home, later writing in one of his autobiographies, *Hitting across the Line* "I did not want to be involved with another county. I needed something else, something pure." Richards brought in the crowds and media scrummages each weekend and the optimistic amateurs within the league looked forward to their own individual battles with the Antiguan. None more so than a certain left arm spinner at Bacup Road. The home game saw a defeat, Richards was out for 31 – caught Barnes, bowled Roscoe. The return fixture at Rishton saw a victory for Rawtenstall. Richards this time made 29 and this time it was stumped Barnes, bowled Roscoe. Peter Denis King (below) was Rawtenstall professional – another Australian form the state of Victoria and he scored 83 to win the game in the 44th over.

King (589 runs) helped the team to a runners-up spot for the first time since 1968. The batting was as consistent as ever with Wood (549), Barlow (459), Pickles (393) and Griffin (364) all scoring well. It was the bowling though that probably cemented the second place. Only four games were lost all season and only four bowlers were used all season – Roscoe (49), Bob Holmes (37), King (34) and Brett Storey (27). Wicketkeeper Peter Barnes also picked up the league award with 37 dismissals in just 15 matches.

Rawtenstall League Runners-up 1987

Back: RJ Singleton (scorer), AC Lawrey, P Pickles, K Roscoe, PD King (pro), G Barlow, B Storey, M Griffin, PS Ashworth.

Seated: J Kershaw, P Barnes, B Terry (capt), PG Wood, R Holmes.

An easy first round win at Nelson in the Worsley Cup saw Roscoe take 6-66 in 20 overs as Nelson finished 169 all out. Rawtenstall had no problem finding the runs and opener Glenn Barlow carried his bat with 74 runs to pass the Nelson total with just four wickets down. The second round game brought Ramsbottom to Bacup Road. Batting first they were all out for 152 with the wickets shared between King, Roscoe and Holmes. Such a score would be relatively easy to make with the batting talent available to Rawtenstall but the Ramsbottom professional, South Australian Andrew Zesers, had other ideas. He ripped through the batting to take 8-32. Rawtenstall were all out for 82.

Despite the success of the previous year King did not return for **1988** instead 25 year old David Norman a South African who represented Natal, was signed. Norman (left) hit 800 runs with seven 50+ scores although he never turned one into a century. That came from Peter Wood – 127 at Burnley in an amazing game that the Burnley side won by just 1 run. Batting first Burnley put 244-5 on the board in the allotted 46 overs with professional Mudassar Nazar hitting 132 and an amateur, who was better known for his exploits at the other Turf Moor - Wales' football international and Burnley FC legend Leighton James, who was no mug with the bat, scored 92. It would be some total to chase but Rawtenstall gave

109

it a go. Wood and Barlow opened and put on 119 for the first wicket – Barlow was out for 52 but Wood continued the partnership with professional Norman putting on another century before Norman was out for 44. Wood made 127 but couldn't quite see the side home to victory. Despite only being four wickets down Rawtenstall lost the game agonisingly by 1 run. However Wood (561), Barlow (547), Kershaw (522) and Griffin (382) made it a bit of a run feast in 1988. The wickets were taken by Norman (58), Roscoe (51), Storey (23) and Holmes (22). It was a good season finishing fourth. The Championship trophy though went to Haslingden. Burnley were the bogey side in the Worsley Cup as well. In the first round game played at Bacup Road, Rawtenstall posted 181-2 in their 48 overs with opener Richard Swift 86 not out and Norman 62 not out. However Mudassar would again be instrumental in the Burnley win with 73 runs as the Turf Moor men reached their target with two overs to spare.

It was back to the Caribbean and Barbados for the final year of the decade and the club signed Anthony Johnson. The Bajan didn't disappoint with 80 wickets including six 5+ wicket games including a match winning 7-42 at Bacup. Roscoe (45) and Holmes (28) also supported Johnson well in the attack. That familiar trio of amateurs did what they had done with the bat throughout the decade Wood (836), Kershaw (693) and Barlow (472) professional Johnson added 457 and Brian Payne 391. Another century came from Wood – 122 not out of 138 balls at home to Accrington. It was another good season and another 4th place. It was a first round exit in the Worsley Cup against Burnley rivals Lowerhouse, who inflicted a heavy defeat at their Liverpool Road ground. The decade though had been good for the club with two Championships, a runners up spot, two 2nd eleven Championships a Worsley cup win, a 2nd eleven cup win and eight top half finishes.

	P	W	L	T	N/R	Bonus pts	Total Pts	Position
1980	26	16	8		2	8	74	3/14
1981	**26**	**17**	**5**		**4**	**12**	**84**	**1/14**
1982	**26**	**17**	**6**		**3**	**10**	**81**	**1/14**
1983	26	9	13		4	4	44	11/14
1984	26	13	10		3	1	56	6/14
1985	26	11	9	1	5	7	58	6/14
1986	26	9	16		1	6	43	13/14
1987	26	14	4		8	7	71	2/14
1988	26	13	9		4	6	62	4/14
1989	26	14	9		3	8	67	4/14

Best seasons of the decade in bold

1990 - 1999 Smells like teen spirit

For the first five years of the decade the Rawtenstall faithful were entertained not only by their own very accomplished amateurs but by two Australian professionals who provided some memorable times to anyone who witnessed their talent. Firstly Colin Miller who features in the first three years followed by two years of Michael Bevan.

The decade started very well with a strong third place behind champions East Lancashire and runners up Haslingden. Miller was an instant success scoring 1078 runs including three centuries at home to Rishton, Church and Accrington. The highest score though went to Peter Wood for his 148 at home against Todmorden. The amateur batting was very strong with Wood (790), 17 year old Andrew Payne (586), Barlow (509) and Brian Payne (387).

The bowling was led by Miller who took 100 wickets. He was the first professional to achieve the double of 1000 runs and 100 wickets since Vijay Hazarre back in 1949. Miller's bowling was complimented by Roscoe (44), Holmes (34), and Storey (24) in fact they took all the wickets bar 5!

Wicketkeeper Peter Barnes with 40 victims broke John Jordan's 1951 record. With such a strong squad most locals felt that a good cup run was on the cards. They weren't wrong as it would be victory for the third time in the Worsley Cup in a not to be forgotten game against local rivals Bacup at Lanehead.

Colin Miller surveys the damage he has just inflicted on the Bacup batsmen in the Worsley Cup Final.

Bacup professional Roger Harper had taken 5-44 on a slow wicket where Wood and Barlow made good 50s apiece. It was then the turn of Miller to produce a match winning performance that has rarely been seen since. Miller tore through the Bacup batsmen taking 9-25 off 20 overs and Bacup were all out for just 79 runs, only Harper offered some resistance.

BACUP C.C. versus RAWTENSTALL C.C.

48 OVERS — Sunday 5th August 1990

BACUP

	BACUP	HOW OUT	BOWLER	RUNS
1	P. THOMPSON (CAPT)	c Barnes	b Miller	0
2	J. HEATON	lbw	b Miller	1
3	P. USHER		b Miller	12
4	T. LORD	c Storey	b Miller	5
5	R. SWIFT	c Kershaw	b Miller	3
6	N. CRONSHAW	c Barnes	b Payne	8
7	P. COOK 10-2-47-0	c + b	Miller	0
8	J. CHAPMAN (WK)	c Holder	b Miller	5
9	D. ORMEROD 6-1-32-2	not out		2
10	J. NUTTALL 18-7-43-0		b Miller	0
11	R. HARPER (PRO) 16-2-46-5	c Kershaw	b Miller	28

Extras: 15
Total: 79 a.o. (39 overs)

Fall of Wicket: 1-2, 2-7, 3-24, 4-41, 5-41, 6-49, 7-72, 8-72, 9-72, 10-79

Runs per Over Summary:

1	2	3	4	5	6	7	8	9	10
1	2	3/1	7/1	20/4	20/4	22/4	7/5	8/5	10/5
11	12	13	14	15	16	17	18	19	20
20/5	20/5	20/5	20/5	20/5	20/5	22/5	22/5	39/5	39/5
21	22	23	24	25	26	27	28	29	30
46/5	46/5	47/5	52/5	54/5	54/5	59/5	60/5	61/5	70/5
31	32	33	34	35	36	37	38	39	40
70/6	72/6	72/6	72/6	72/9	72/9	72/9	73/9	79 a.o.	
41	42	43	44	45	46	47	48		

RAWTENSTALL

	BACUP	HOW OUT	BOWLER	RUNS
1	B. TERRY (CAPT)	c Lord	b Harper	2
2	P. WOOD	c Chapman	b Ormerod	50
3	G. BARLOW		b Harper	52
4	G. HOLDER	not out		2
5	A. PAYNE 6-2-3-1	lbw	b Harper	3
6	J. KERSHAW	run out		35
7	B. STOREY 15-4-43-0		b Harper	9
8	R. HOLMES		b Harper	2
9	K. ROSCOE	not out		2
10	P. BARNES (WK)	(d.n.b)		
11	C. MILLER (PRO) 20-9-25-9		b Ormerod	7

Extras: 21
Total: 185-8 (48 overs)

Fall of Wicket: 1-105, 2-111, 3-117, 4-146, 5-155, 6-177, 7-181, 8-183

Runs per Over Summary:

1	2	3	4	5	6	7	8	9	10
4	5	6	13	14	15	21	37	38	38
11	12	13	14	15	16	17	18	19	20
39	41	41	41	41	46	46	50	51	62
21	22	23	24	25	26	27	28	29	30
68	68	73	75	75	79	84	86	89	90
31	32	33	34	35	36	37	38	39	40
97	101	105/1	111/1	117/2	119/2	123/4	123/4	129/4	134/4
41	42	43	44	45	46	47	48		
146/5	153/6	155/6	157/5	162/6	172/6	179/6	185/8		

Gate: £1,958.00 (£1.50/15p)

Collections:
P. Wood — £95
G. Barlow — £80
C. Miller — £75

Man of the Match (Amateur): J. Kershaw.

Above is the scorecard from the Worsley Cup final. The gate of £1,958 would be worth £4,000 today. Similarly the collections for Wood, £95 (£195) Barlow £80 (£165) and Miller £75 (£155) would be handsome rewards.

One of Miller's nine wickets - Bacup's John Nuttall watches his middle stump fly through the air.

In **1991** Miller again had a good season but it would be the exploits of an amateur batsman that would make the headlines. Peter Wood hit an amazing 1227 runs with two centuries and eleven 50+ scores. It was a year for batsmen as Peter Sleep, another Australian professional, broke Everton Weekes' run aggregate in the league amassing 1621 league runs. There was more success as John Kershaw (below) with 625 runs had his best season and a memorable 141 not out at home to East Lancashire – the highest amateur score of the season. Glenn Barlow also added another 450 runs to the pot.

There was plenty of quality batting but the bowling lacked depth. Miller with 108 wickets bettered his previous year's performance with 9-31 at home to Burnley being particularly memorable - but only the left arm spin of Roscoe (33) offered any back up. The old adage "Bowlers win Matches" was oh so true as a mid-table position would be all that was attained.

113

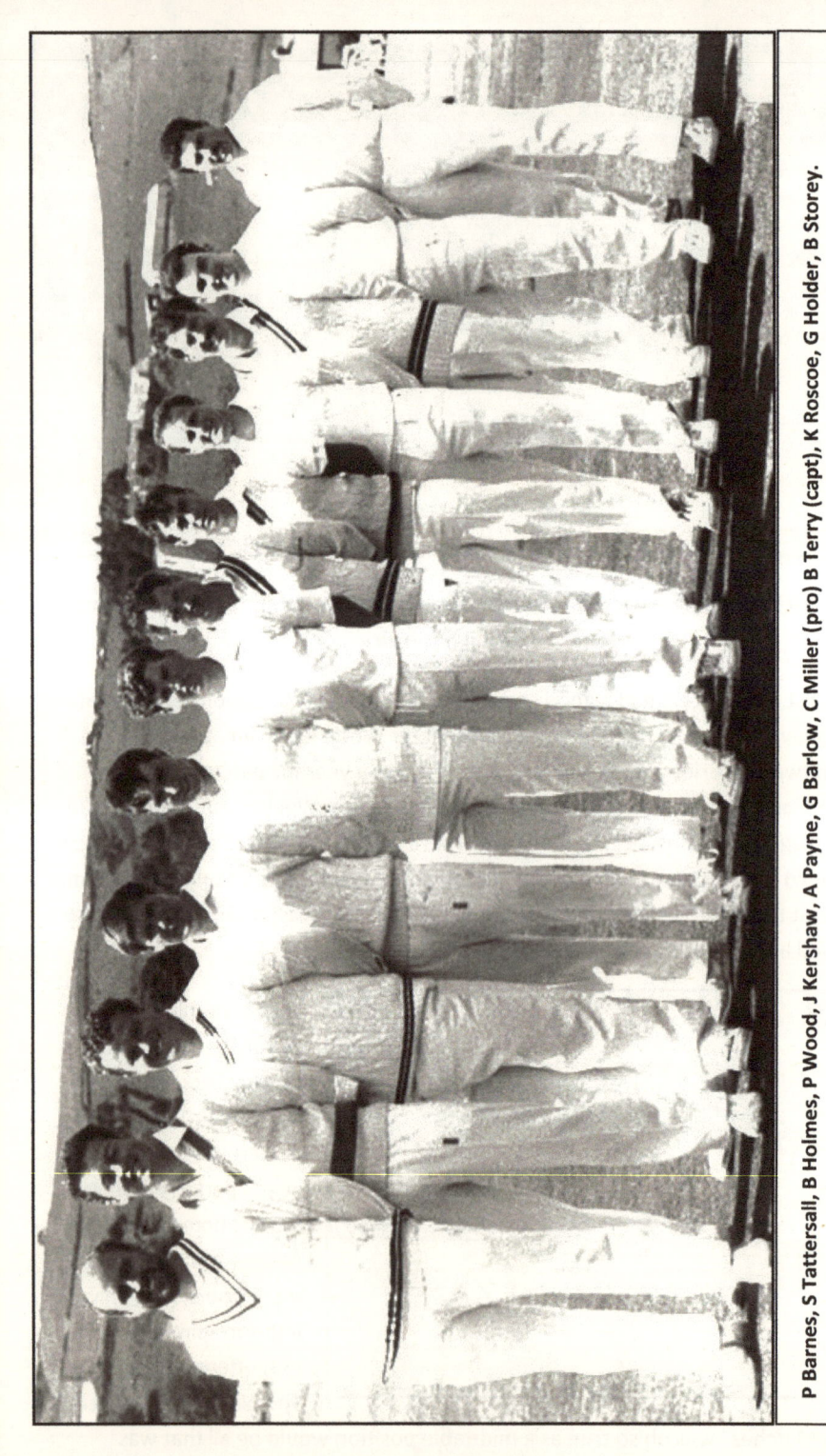

P Barnes, S Tattersall, B Holmes, P Wood, J Kershaw, A Payne, G Barlow, C Miller (pro) B Terry (capt), K Roscoe, G Holder, B Storey.

Rawtenstall Worsley Cup Winners 1990

Miller's last season was **1992** and there was no repeat of his exploits of the previous two seasons. With the advancement of home cinema and videos the local cinema 'The Picture House' was nearing its end as another operator took over. There were no Oscars to show off at Bacup Road either as another mid-table finish would complete Miller's 3 year stint. The runs came from the usual suspects: Wood (646), Kershaw (514), Miller (405) and Barlow (333). It was the Miller/Roscoe show with the ball - 75 and 54 wickets respectively. Colin Reid Miller (right), played 18 Tests for Australia between 1998 and 2001. He was a bowler capable of performing effectively either as a right arm fast-medium or off break bowler and achieved a Test average of 26.15. A tail end batsman who made three fifties in 126 first-class matches.

1993 saw another third place finish in a very close campaign. Rawtenstall had the same points as second place Ramsbottom but were runners up on account of the number of games won. Haslingden won the title by just 3 points. The latest Australian to join the list of great Rawtenstall antipodeans was Michael Gwyl Bevan (below). In future years he would be known as one of the world's best limited overs batsmen. Luckily for the Rawtenstall faithful they saw his young talent prior to his introduction on the international stage. Bevan at just 20 years of age was one of the finest batsmen ever seen at Bacup Road. It was the year that Bevan (1344), Peter Wood (719) and John Kershaw (609) dominated the batting in the league. The bowling of Bevan (62), Peter Seal (41) and Robert Holmes (39) formed the nucleus of the attack. In fact just four bowlers took all the league wickets that season, Pat Rush (21) being the other contributor. Bevan was particularly awesome and ruthless. A record 2nd wicket partnership of 227 against

Lowerhouse with Peter Wood (107) and Bevan (142) was just one of the many batting displays served up. Wood and Kershaw also got in on the act with a 190 partnership versus Rishton.

Another well remembered game that season, especially if you find yourself in the company of Robert Holmes 'mine host' at the Red Lion in Higher Cloughfold, was the game at Accrington on 14th August.

Rawtenstall had scored 205 -2 with Wood, Bevan (above) Kershaw and Barlow all contributing. When Accrington batted, Holmes, with his medium pace, tore through the line-up ensuring no-one reached double figures. Accrington were skittled out for just 45 runs and Holmes had the amazing figures of: **12.2 overs, 3 maidens, 17 runs, 8 wickets.** It was the best amateur bowling performance of the season and won him the merited Lancashire Evening Telegraph Tankard and, at the time, was the third best amateur league bowling performance. Only Howarth (1916) and Banks (1940) had a better return.

In the Worsley Cup it would be a repeat of the 1990 final after victories over Accrington and Church – Bevan (124) and a nail biting 3 run semi-final win over Enfield (Bevan 144). This time Rawtenstall were at home and confidence was high. Batting first, Bevan scored 91 in a total of 192 -8 off 50 overs. It was never going to be enough and Bacup won at a canter, losing just one wicket in 40 overs with a partnership of 166 between amateur opener Mark Taylor (62 not out) and Bacup's West Indian professional - Roger Harper (104 not out). The gate was £3295 for a £2 entrance. Today it would be worth over £5000.

Bevan was only able to play just over half of the season's games for **1994**. Despite this he was able to score 756 runs and take 43 wickets. He signed off with two centuries at home to Accrington and Rishton and his best bowling performance 7-15 at Lowerhouse.

After setting a record breaking second wicket the previous season Bevan and Wood broke it again. The match in question was at home to Rishton on 29th May. Rawtenstall batted first and posted 268-1 with Peter Wood 126 not out and Bevan

118 not out. Veteran Australian test player Peter Sleep was professional for Rishton and had bowling figures of 1-100 off 19 overs. However 3 years earlier Sleep had broken Everton Weekes League record batting aggregate with 1621 runs and was no mug with the bat. When the rain arrived his 83 not out in a total of 223-3 off 34 overs meant amazingly that Rishton had won the game on run rate!

Peter Wood (656), Steve Tattersall (346) and Glenn Barlow (318) scored the runs and Bob Holmes had his best season with the ball taking 40 wickets including 7-51 away at Church who were 138 all out. However Rawtenstall ended up all out for 83 with Church amateur John Longden taking 9-46. Having to play the last 10 games with sub-pros, including Lancashire's Ian Austin, affected the team and a final finish of 11th was disappointing.

After five years of scintillating cricket from Australians Miller and Bevan the next five would prove to be a challenging and difficult time for the team.

Rawtenstall turned to South Africa for their paid man for **1995**. Ross Edward Veenstra (right), played just 15 games for the club before having to return home due to injury. With 391 runs and 38 wickets he wasn't exactly setting the world on fire. Substitute professionals included the return of Franklyn Stephenson and his countryman, Eldine Baptiste.

Stephen Tattersall (460) was leading amateur batsman followed closely by Glenn Barlow (442) and 377 from Peter Wood who played 16 games. The bowling attack was led by Richard Glover (30) and Pat Rush (29) but lacked any real pace and penetration. Losing 20 of the 26 games played, Rawtenstall just avoided the wooden spoon finishing above Accrington in 13th place.

The team did reach the semi-final of the cup. After a first round bye they faced Ramsbottom at home in the second round. Rawtenstall posted 173 in their 50 overs with Veenstra top scoring with 47. Replying Ramsbottom edged closer to the total but fell short by just 6 runs. The bowling heroes for Rawtenstall were Pat Rush with 4-61, Veenstra with 3-50 and Dawson with 2-26. The semi-final was up the road at Haslingden. Rawtenstall were all out for 176 despite a battling 68 from Peter Wood. It was Australian test bowler and Haslingden professional, Paul

Reiffel who was Haslingdens star, taking 7-48 ....All clean bowled! Haslingden reached the total in less than 40 overs with amateur Graham Knowles 91 not out.

1996 saw the appointment of the second Zimbabwean professional to represent the club Guy James Whittall (below). However despite some strong individual performances it was pretty much a repeat of the previous season.

Whittall played 20 matches, and with 637 runs with five x 50+ scores and 51 wickets including 8-30 at East Lancashire, performed reasonably well.

The batting was well supported by Peter Wood (643), Glenn Barlow (434), Richard Wood (411), and sub-pro Peter Sleep who hit 357 runs in six matches! The bowling though offered little support with Rush (21) and Glover (20) the leading amateurs. It would be another 13th place in the league, just above Accrington.

In the cup an unlikely first round win at Lowerhouse also unearthed an unlikely hero. Rawtenstall could anly score 103. But Lowerhouse were skittled out for 74. Whittall took 3-32 but the real star was Tony Greenwood whose only other appreance for the club was way back in 1968. Greenwood took the last three Lowerhouse wickets to fall and ended up with the remarkable figures of:
5 overs, 2 maidens, 4 runs, 3 wickets.

The second round tie was at home to Ramsbottom. It was their New Zealand professional Chis Harris with a faultless all-round display that would determine the outcome of the game. Ramsbotom were 187 all out with Harris scoring 83 . Despite three Rawtenstall batsmen contributing 121 runs in reply – Whittall (48), P Wood (38) and R Wood (35) the other eight couldn't score the other 66 runs between them. Rawtenstall were all out for 153. Harris took 5-70 with the ball and Ramsbottom went on to win the cup in a close final at Bacup.

The season would also be the last for Peter Wood who signed off with 14,926 league runs over 24 seasons plus another 1200 in the cup. Rawtenstall's all time leading run scorer by some considerable margin, with twelve 100's and ninety nine 50+ scores. A 50+ score or more on each Lancashire League ground and a century against eight of the 13 opposing teams. He also scored 99 not out against Bacup and 98 v Colne!

Peter Wood's League batting record for Rawtenstall

Year	Matches	Innings	N/O	Runs	Highest	Ave	100	50
1968	8	2	1	19	17	19.00	0	0
1971	20	19	2	338	60	19.88	0	2
1972	16	15	2	150	40	11.53	0	0
1973	23	22	4	458	66	25.44	0	2
1974	22	21	3	657	72*	36.50	0	5
1976	26	25	3	732	82*	33.27	0	4
1977	21	20	2	494	100	27.44	1	2
1978	23	23	3	912	103*	45.60	1	8
1979	22	22	3	489	49	25.73	0	0
1980	24	24	4	917	108	45.85	1	8
1981	22	22	4	687	81*	38.16	0	6
1984	22	20	3	594	65*	34.94	0	4
1985	23	22	4	707	80*	39.27	0	6
1986	23	23	0	768	91	33.39	0	8
1987	19	18	2	549	99*	34.31	0	4
1988	19	19	2	561	127	33.00	1	2
1989	23	23	3	836	122*	41.80	1	6
1990	23	23	5	790	**148**	43.88	1	5
1991	25	25	2	**1227**	131	**53.34**	2	11
1992	22	22	0	646	105	29.36	1	4
1993	25	25	2	719	107	31.26	2	2
1994	23	23	2	656	126*	31.23	1	2
1995	16	16	0	377	79	23.56	0	4
1996	23	23	0	643	81	27.95	0	4

Peter Wood

The club went back to Australia in **1997** in an attempt to re-capture the success of the earlier part of the decade. Ian Stephen Louis Hewitt (left), a 21 year old left handed batsman and bowler from Victoria State. It proved to be a steep learning curve for the young Australian who only managed to score 238 runs and take 32 wickets in 18 games before returning home. Some of the enlightened Rawtenstall fans felt it was his performances off the field that led to him returning home rather quicker than anticipated.

There was though one memorable game for the young Aussie and it took place at home against Ramsbottom on on 14th June. Rawtenstall batting first could only make 104 -9 from their 46 overs. In reply Hewett produced one of the best bowling displays to be seen at Bacup Road for quite some time.

Hewitt finished up with the figures of: **15.3 overs, 5 maidens, 27 runs, 8 wickets.**

The last six matches were played by test stars Keith Arthurton and Nathan Astle. Only four games were won throughout the season. Barlow (404) and John Hall (322) were the only significant scorers.

There was a batting partnership record though and it was for the seventh wicket. It was between Glenn Barlow and Pat Rush and took place on 20th July against Accrington at home. Rush made 48 and Barlow carried his bat through the innings for 101 not out as Rawtenstall posted 188. But it was that man Sleep who again came to torment the Rawtenstall faithful with 87 not out to win for Accrington in a game which proved to be Hewitt's last for the club.

Roscoe, having returned to Lancashire League action after a five year break playing in the North East and as professional for Edenfield in the Ribblesdale League, was leading bowler with 36 scalps and the wooden spoon hung from the changing room wall.

In **1998** the West Indies test star Keith Lloyd Thomas Arthurton was professional. After some useful performances as sub professional the previous year, the left hander from the tiny Leeward Island of Nevis didn't disappoint with the bat scoring 1156 runs including six centuries and five 50+ scores. His highest century and the second highest score in the league that year was 137 not out at Enfield. His 50 came off 50 balls in 50 minutes and his 100 off just 110 deliveries. However there was little support coming from the amateur batters. No-one scored over 50 in a game with Glenn Barlow (319) the only man to score over 300 runs.

The top bowler was Roscoe (62) with a leading performance of 7-45, which won him the Evening Telegraph bowling tankard in the home game against Nelson. However Roscoe would end up on the losing team as Rawtenstall were all out 35 runs short of the Nelson total of 156. Arthurton (left) chipped in with 27 wickets but that was it. Then again, it was an improvement and a better season than the previous three.

The last season in the decade and the millennium saw the club turn to South African Lloyd Ferriera, however he didn't last half the season. He did manage to score 439 runs in 12 games including a memorable win against Church at home. Church batted first and put 257 on the scoreboard. Ferriera took the Church bowling apart scoring 154 not out and winning the game in the last over. Sub-professionals were employed for the rest of the campaign.

James Anderson

A young 16 year old fast bowler from Burnley was starting his cricket career in the Lancashire League in 1999 and in the May game against Rawtenstall at Turf Moor he had figures of 0-19 of 6 overs. It was another bowler who took the plaudits as Keith Roscoe finished with 6-27 and Burnley were skittled out for 84. The return fixture in July saw victory for Burnley with Anderson taking 2-36 of 9 overs.... including 7 wides! No-one had any idea that they were watching a future Lancashire player who would also become England's leading wicket taker.

Wicketkeeper Peter Vincent Hanson (450) had his best season with the bat and was supported by Peter Seal (395). Roscoe (56) and Seal (36) took the most wickets but despite winning eight games, the team finished bottom of the league.

	P	W	L	D	N/R	T	Bonus	Pts	Position
1990	26	19	7		0		9	85	3/14
1991	26	15	11		0		8	68	7/14
1992	26	10	11		5		7	52	8/14
1993	26	18	6		2		9	83	3/14
1994	26	8	17		1		10	43	11/14
1995	26	5	20		1		3	24	13/14
1996	26	6	19		1		5	31	13/14
1997	26	4	18		2	2	3	27	14/14
1998	26	4	7	9	6		18	88	12/14
1999	26	8	17		1		32	114	14/14

Best seasons of the decade in bold

2000 – 2009 Beautiful Day

After the disappointment of the previous year the Rawtenstall faithful needed a pick-me-up as we greeted the new millennium.

They got it from their left arm spinner Keith Roscoe. It proved to be the club's best ever wicket taking performance in a season by an amateur. It overtook by some way Tom Waller's 71 wickets in 1921 and Bob Banks 70 wickets in 1952. Indeed the club record still stands today. Roscoe took 91 wickets including nine 5 + wicket hauls and a best of 8-25 at home to Rishton. He was the second leading bowler in the league behind the prolific Bacup professional Adam Dale who took 109 wickets.

The season started with the club finding another popular Australian who would once again score some big 100's. Matthew Peter Mott (right), a batsman from Queensland surpassed his compatriots Miller and Bevan hitting 1317 league runs. With three centuries and nine 50+ scores he dominated the Rawtenstall batting statistics so much so that Peter Hanson (336) was the only other batsman to score more than 250 runs. Hanson also had an excellent season behind the stumps claiming 46 victims (22 caught and 24 stumped). Mott took 39 wickets and Peter Seal 38 but the batting needed strengthening, especially as long serving opener Glenn Barlow (left) announced his retirement.

Barlow's 25 year record totalled 10,245 league runs. He also amassed over 1000 runs in the 43 Worsley Cup games. The second highest run scorer for the club - his league figures are highlighted below:

Matches	Innings	Not Out	Runs	Highest	Ave	100	50	Catches
524	507	53	10245	126*	22.5	6	45	131

2001 saw the passing of former England, Lancashire and Rawtenstall batsman Winston Place who loved his home town and loved his cricket.

A top six place was achieved mainly due to Mott who bettered his previous year's runs total with 1391. He had better support from Andrew Payne – returning after a few years with Somerset County Cricket Club. Payne hit 406 runs and Peter Hanson 355. Payne offered more balance to the bowling attack as well. The wickets were shared between Payne (42), Mott (38), Roscoe (38) and Seal (25).

A record eighth wicket partnership between Mott and AJ Clough also occurred in the season. At home to Burnley, Rawtenstall were 89-7 when Andrew Clough came to the crease to support Mott. The pair put on 101 runs to help Rawtenstall make a score of 194, Mott finishing 115 not out. Burnley were 149 all out and Rawtenstall won by 45 runs. Admittedly Clough would appear higher in the batting order over the next few seasons, but at the time his 26 runs were his highest score for the club.

Mott later in his career coached Glamorgan County Cricket Club and more recently has been in charge of the Australian Women's' Team.

Future South African test and 1 day international Andrew Hall (left) was recruited as professional for the **2002** season. Hall had a good season with the bat scoring 723 runs including two centuries at home to Burnley and Accrington. Payne was also in the runs hitting 643 and his first century, also in the game against Burnley where the partnership with Hall was 166.

18 year old Chris Cook-Martin showed his potential with 331 and Richard Wood also hit his one and only century for the club, 102 not out chasing and beating the 250 posted by Rishton. Hall struggled with the ball though taking just 33 wickets. Roscoe (58) followed by Payne (28) and John Dawson (27) were the other main wicket takers as a mid-table 7th place was achieved.

There was more success for the club – twenty two years since the inception of a Lancashire League third eleven, 2002 saw Rawtenstall win the championship for their first, and currently only, time.

South Australian, Mike John Smith arrived in **2003** and lasted 19 games before returning home with an injury. He scored 632 runs with two centuries against Rishton both home and away. The batting though was dominated by Andrew

Payne, who not only hit 1181 runs but also scored his highest ever individual score. It was the highest score in the league that year and standing at no1 as the highest score ever made by a Rawtenstall player. It took place at home on 7th September against Nelson. Payne (below) hit 173 in a total of 337 -7, the highest limited overs score ever seen at the Worswick Memorial Ground at that time. Chris Cook-Martin nearly doubled his run aggregate from the previous season with 601 runs. Richard Wood (368) and Peter Hanson (290) both contributed well. The bowling didn't match the batting performances and only Roscoe (41) and Smith (32) provided any impact. In Roscoe's 41 wickets though was a performance that would re-write the clubs record book.

Roscoe made history as the first amateur bowler to take nine wickets in an innings since Fred Haworth did ninety years ago in 1916 - indeed they are the only two Rawtenstall amateurs to ever achieve this feat. It happened at the oldest ground in the league – The Horsfield, home of Colne CC on the 26th July. It was a game of highlights, firstly 111 not out by opener Andrew Payne in a Rawtenstall total of 215 -7. Colne looked as though they were going to win and were 156-3 before Roscoe took control. The last seven wickets went for just 29 runs, all to Roscoe, including a hat-trick.

His analysis was: **24.5 overs, 7 Maidens, 9 wickets for 77 runs**

Popular wicketkeeper and captain Peter Hanson featured strongly in a classic game at home to Church on 20th July. It would become the second highest seventh wicket partnership for the club. Church put 229 on the board and Rawtenstall were practically dead and buried at 78-6 when Hanson joined Daniel Barlow at the crease. The keeper proceeded to score his highest ever league score (93 not out), and with Barlow (47) in a partnership of 111, secured a victory that no-one would have predicted.

The highlight of the season though was winning the Worsley Cup for the fourth time. It was a particular triumph for Smith who performed well in each round. A first round win over Nelson saw Smith hit 129 and take 5-30. Smith was at it again at home to Burnley in the 2nd round making 73 not out and chasing down the Turf Moor club's score of 223. The semi-final was away at Colne where Payne this time dominated the batting hitting 147 in a total of 316-6 off the allotted 50 overs. It was the highest ever score by a Rawtenstall player in a Worsley Cup game. Colne got nowhere near and Rawtenstall were off to Blackburn to face East Lancashire in the final.

Smith (left) was unavailable for the final due to injury so Lancashire all-rounder Ian Austin stood in as sub-professional. Rawtenstall won the toss and batted with Payne (60) and Cook-Martin (70) establishing a solid foundation. A score of 223-7 was made. The East Lancashire side was never in the game and was skittled out for just 89 runs. Roscoe (4-17), Austin (2-14), Seal (2-25) and one wicket apiece for Dawson and Payne were the wicket takers and the celebrations could begin.

Rawtenstall players celebrate winning The Worsley Cup

Rawtenstall Worsley Cup Winners 2003

Top Row: Afrus Ali, Andrew Clough, John Dawson, Keith Roscoe.

Middle Row: Daniel Barlow, Peter V Hanson (capt), Chris Cook-Martin.

Front Row: Andrew Payne, Ian Austin (sub pro), Richard Wood, Peter Seal.

For the next two years Rawtenstall turned to 'one of their own' as their professional. You would have to go back to 1979 and see Alan Worsick as the last Englishman in a paid capacity. It was a popular appointment and, as the statistics prove, Andrew Payne was more than competent in the role.

2004 provided some memorable moments none more so than on 24th August. In the history of Rawtenstall Cricket Club only nine players have managed to score a century and take five wickets or more in a league game. Eight of those men were professionals. The only amateur to achieve this feat was Peter Seal on the 24th August 2004 against Colne. Rawtenstall batted first with Seal and professional Andrew Payne opening. A stand of 96 set the platform to enable Seal to make his only century for the club scoring 101 in a total of 201-7. Replying, Colne also started well with a 50 partnership for the first wicket. Seal then struck, and in tandem with Keith Roscoe went on to bowl Colne out for 178. Seal's figures were: **16 overs, 3 maidens, 5 wickets for 68 runs.**

There were some excellent batting performances throughout the year. Payne led the way with 910 runs, but four amateurs also scored over 400 runs for the season. Wood (480), Seal (470), Cook-Martin (460) and Hanson (444) ensured it wasn't just a one man show. Three men took most of the wickets – Roscoe (66), Payne (55) and Seal (45) and an encouraging 4th place was achieved.

There was no repeat of the Worsley Cup triumph of the previous year. This time it was a first round exit at East Lancashire.

At the end of season League Dinner, Roscoe was presented with a special award from the League President - Malcolm Heywood (below) upon achieving 1000 Lancashire League wickets.

The following year wasn't quite as impressive although Payne again was scoring freely; hitting 759 runs including 104 not out at Accrington. Cook-Martin had his best season to date with 581 whilst 358 from John Hayman was also encouraging. Bowling- wise, Roscoe was in fine form with 84 scalps. Payne took 47 and Seal 22 wickets but consistency was in short supply and 7th place would be where the team would finish.

Following the success of 20/20 cricket across the country the league introduced a competition for the clubs played on Friday evenings. It was a short lived experience for the Rawtenstall team who were eliminated at home against East Lancashire in the first round.

The doors on the most ambitious shopping centre seen in Rossendale for years were set to open in May **2006** it was announced in the Rossendale Free Press. The Heritage Arcade development, at the former Picture House cinema, had been transformed at massive cost to house 19 shops, a restaurant and a cafe and would link in with a new retail centre being created in the old Kwik Save store on Bacup Road. A number of traders were negotiating moving into the old cinema. "How long would it last?" muttered a few of the Rawtenstall cynics. "Perhaps as long as their Australian paid man could stay at the crease," replied another. Now Rawtenstall have had some fine Australian professionals who have performed magnificently over the years. One thinks back to Ken Grieves, George Tribe, John Grant, Colin Miller, Michael Bevan and Matthew Mott – however Alan Brett Wise (right) is unlikely to ever feature in such a distinguished list.

Wise was a left arm fast medium bowler and did take 53 wickets in his 26 matches. It is though expected that paid men can 'bat a bit' but Wise was ignorant in all aspects of batsmanship. He scored just 113 runs with a top score of 19. Thankfully the usual suspects, Payne (566), Cook-Martin (468) and Seal (380) did their bit but it would never be enough. The amateur bowlers also struggled – Roscoe (33), Payne (24), and Seal (22).

In the cup there was a first round win at Lowerhouse. Posting 170-9 on the board with Daniel Barlow top scoring with 57, the Rawtenstall bowlers had something to bowl against especially as Lowerhouse had a strong batting line up. It proved the case but Rawtenstall kept at it and won by just 6 runs. Wise took 3-17 off 10 overs. The second round game at Bacup Road saw East Lancashire visiting. Batting first, Payne scored a century (113) in Rawtenstall's formidable total of 224-7.

However the East Lancashire amateur stalwarts David Pearson (73 not out) and Phil Mercer (80 not out) saw them reach the total with 4 overs left.

There needed to be some wise and considered thinking on the part of the committee to rectify what had been a very disheartening season.

It had been 29 years since Rawtenstall had turned to India to find their professional and what a good one he was! So optimism was high when Sanjay Bapusaheb Bangar was appointed for **2007**. Bangar (above) missed the first four matches and took some time to settle in as Rawtenstall found themselves at the wrong end of the table. In fact the club languished in 12th spot when they embarked on an unbeaten run that saw them win ten matches in a row after beating Ramsbottom at Acre Bottom on July 8th in the only match to be played on that day. Bangar's match winning performance saw him score the first of seven half centuries in his total of 674 runs at 51.8.

Perhaps of more significance was his switch to bowling off spin which saw him pick up 56 wickets at 18.7.

The batting performances came from Cook-Martin (625), including his first century 108 at Burnley. Payne (589) with 119 at home to East Lancashire and 20 year old Daniel Barlow who continued where his father had finished off with an encouraging 390 runs. Roscoe, with 58, was the leading wicket taker and it was an unforeseen runner-up spot behind Rishton.

Rawtenstall League Runners Up 2007

Back: W Cook-Martin, P Hanson, P Seal, K Roscoe, G King, J Dawson, A Riley

Front: C Cook-Martin, S Bangar (pro), A Payne (capt), A Ali, D Barlow.

Bangar would not be returning as Rawtenstall professional for **2008** as the all-rounder's wife was expecting a baby in the summer. This was the unfortunate press release that greeted the Rawtenstall faithful. Chairman Brian Payne said: "It's a big disappointment. Sanjay has been in touch with us every week and he had been looking forward to coming back."

The club quickly turned to their first ever New Zealand professional all-rounder Nathan McCullum It was the amateurs though who dominated the season - firstly Payne with 871 runs including nine 50+ scores. Matching him was Cook-Martin with 836 runs and two centuries, 105 at Todmorden at the end of June, and 104 at Lowerhouse in late August. McCullum (right), scored 431 in 20 games and Daniel Barlow 332. All the wickets bar eight were shared by just three bowlers. Roscoe 71- including his 1000th wicket for the club - McCullum 70 and Payne 49. Wicketkeeper Hanson also picked up 31 victims.

In the 20/20 competition Rawtenstall had some success for the first time. The game was now based on mini- leagues and all the valley sides plus Edenfield from the Ribblesdale League made up the group of five teams. Rawtenstall topped their group and faced Burnley in the semi-final at Bacup Road but the Turf Moor men won easily, although they lost to East Lancashire in the final.

The final season in the decade saw the club return to Andrew Payne as the paid man who scored 612 runs and took 41 wickets. The leading batsman and amateur bowler was Toby Bulcock who had just one season with the club. Bulcock scored 625 runs and took 30 wickets. 18 year old Joshua Rushmore was the only player to score a century. It occurred in the match at home against Lowerhouse. Batting first Rawtenstall put 256-8 on the board which would be a good score for any team to match. Rushmore made 104 and Payne 71. Lowerhouse though had a strong batting line-up themselves and it was their amateur Chis Bleazard scoring 119 that was instrumental in enabling the Burnley based side to win in the last over. Rushmore scored 345 runs for the season in support of Bulcock and Payne. The wickets were shared between Bulcock (30), Shafiq (28) and Roscoe (26). Despite seven victories it was a disappointing end to the decade with the team finishing bottom of the league.

	P	W	L	N/R	Bonus		Pts	Position
2000	26	10	15	1	40		143	11/14
2001	26	11	10	5	37		162	5/14
2002	26	11	9	6	18		146	7/14
2003	26	10	15	1	30		135	12/14
2004	26	14	9	3	43		192	4/14
					Bonus bat	Bonus Bowl		
2005	26	13	12	1	10	27	170	7/14
2006	26	5	14	7	7	29	107	12/14
2007	**26**	**14**	**7**	**5**	**5**	**24**	**184**	**2/14**
2008	**23**	**16**	**8**	**2**	**10**	**38**	**214**	**2/14**
2009	26	7	17	2	3	27	106	14/14

Best seasons of the decade in bold

2010 - 2019 Price Tag

The decade would prove to be a difficult one for the club both on and off the field. Up to this time the best seasons have been mid-table achievements. The difficulty of securing a professional who would last the season was a defining point, but also the loss of key amateur players would be crucial. However the decade would also see six of the best batting partnerships witnessed and recorded in the club's history.

The decade started reasonably well with a mid-table finish. Professional was Pakistani Naved Arif (below) 769 runs and 64 wickets including 8-35 at home to Lowerhouse. Arif's performances quickly attracted the interests of Sussex CC where he spent the following two years.

The first game of the season away at Enfield ended up as a tie. Enfield posted 147 with Rawtenstall sub-professional Bilal Khilji taking 6-42. Rawtenstall replied with Andrew Clough making 55 but no other batsman scored above 15.

There were some strong amateur performances with the bat. A Payne 896, J Rushmore 518 and A Clough 661, being particularly proficient. Roscoe took 73 wickets including 7-89 in a close game at home to Bacup. With statistics like this you would have thought that they would have been challenging at the top but there was no consistency.

The **2011** season saw the club venture into new pastures with their first Sri-Lankan professional. It should have been Malinga Bandra but he would have had to return home in July due to contractual obligations. The club quickly appointed Nilantha Cooray who came as a right hand batsman and leg break bowler.

In the 18 matches that he played for the club Cooray scored 609 runs at 43.5 with an unbeaten 114 in a partnership of 193 with Payne (73 not out) against East Lancashire his highest score. He also put on a club record 4th wicket stand of 200 with Andrew Payne in an epic win over Ramsbottom at Rawtenstall. The game in question took place at home on 31st July. Ramsbottom batted first, putting 306 on the board for just 5 wickets with New Zealand professional Shanan Stewart making 150 of them. Rawtenstall made a steady start and were 110 -3 with Kerrigan (42) and Clough (51) before Cooray (left) and Payne put together their 200 partnership. Victory was secured in the 44th over in what was one of the finest partnerships ever witnessed at Bacup Road.

Roscoe led with the ball again with 72 wickets, Cooray took 33 and Rizwan Shafiq 25. Payne led the way with the bat scoring 658 runs including 103 not out in the game against Ramsbottom. J Kerrigan (435) and Clough (357) were the other main contributors. Kerrigan also hit his one and only century in his only season with the club exactly 100 in the home defeat to Accrington. As with last season there was no consistency. Other sub professionals used were Brett Pelser and Lou Vincent who featured in another impressive partnership this time with Andrew Clough. The game was against Burnley at Turf Moor on the opening game of the season. Vincent (108) and Clough (92) made the third highest 2nd wicket partnership for the club (209) in a total of 292 -5. Roscoe then took 7-33 off 19 overs to secure an opening day win by more than 100 runs.

South African Jandre Coetzee was signed for **2012** but again was another paid man who didn't last the full term. Coetzee (right), had played for Central Lancashire League club Walsden back in 2006 scoring 841 runs and taking 88 wickets. He obviously was familiar with League conditions and seemed a good signing. However he didn't bring his credentials from Walsden to Rawtenstall. He played in 19 games and scored just 220 runs. Leading scorer was Matt Kershaw with 339 whilst no other batsmen hit more than 250. Coetzee took 43 wickets and Roscoe 53. Just four games were won and the club would finish bottom of the league.

If 2012 was a difficult year then **2013** was finally a year when some consistency in the professional lasting the full term was achieved. The club signed Bret Pelser another South African who had had a degree of success with other league clubs.

Pelser not only provided some extra stability to the club but also performed well on and off the field organising practice and coaching the juniors.

Pelser (right), hit 834 league runs with four centuries126 at home to Church, 119 not out away at Colne, 109 not out at Ramsbottom and 109 away at Todmorden. Eighteen year old Sam Kershaw was leading amateur with 403 with solid contributions coming from Peter Wrathmell (386) and Chris Cook- Martin (324). The bowling was shared between Roscoe (53), off spinner Imran Abid (44), Pelser (41) and 25 from Rizwan Shafiq. Despite finishing in eleventh place it was a positive season in many ways.

The batting partnership for the season belonged to Pelser and Peter Wrathmell. It was the second highest fifth wicket partnership in the club's history and took place at Bacup Road versus Colne. The game was on the 27th July. Chasing Colne's 191, Rawtenstall were 53-4 and in trouble. However, Pelser (57 not out) and Wrathmell (69 not out) put together a fifth wicket partnership of 141 to secure victory. It was the second highest fifth wicket partnership, and only 10 runs short of the record held by H Greenwood and RH Whittaker back in 1950.

Pelser returned for **2014** and improved his aggregate with 859 runs. He scored just one century 101 not out at home against Nelson. The amateurs though also responded well with Cook-Martin hitting 584 including a century - a big one - 145 at home to East Lancashire. Sam Kershaw again was improving with 536 and Dean Barlow (363) all had their moments. Roscoe (78), Pelser (47) and Shafiq (27) took the wickets. Wicketkeeper and captain Hanson, who was playing his last full season, had his best year since 2000 with 40 victims (25 caught and 15 stumped). The derby game at Bacup also witnessed the third best sixth wicket partnership in the club's history (102). It was created by Pelser (62 not out) and George Bevan (50 not out). Won 13.... Lost 13 and, as you have guessed, a mid-table league position.

In the Worsley Cup there was an extraordinary first round home game against Rishton. Rawtenstall batted first and Peter Hanson opened the batting and proceeded to hit 125 and share a second wicket partnership of 177 with Chris Cook-Martin. It would be Hanson's one and only century in his 20 year career. Rawtenstall finished on 301-7 off their 50 overs and 99% of those present thought "game over". However Rishton had other ideas and an eighth wicket partnership of 55 edged them closer to the Rawtenstall total but the overs ran out and Rishton at 299-9 were just 2 runs short.

In the second round another victory came – this time at Ramsbottom. Rawtenstall made 220-6 with Pelser scoring 86 and Sam Kershaw 46. All the Rawtenstall bowlers bowled tight but it was Roscoe with 5-34 that took the plaudits. The semi-final was at home to Lowerhouse and for those who witnessed it would see one of the best modern day games played at Bacup Road. Lowerhouse made 224-9 in their 50 overs with Andy Riley taking 4-40. Rawtenstall replied with a fine 80 runs from opener Cook-Martin then 63 from middle order man Peter Wrathmell, however the wickets kept coming. An excellent 27 from no.9 batsman Cameron Holder kept everyone on their seat. The ninth wicket fell at 223 Roscoe joined his fellow spinner Imran Abid at the wicket who proceeded to hit the winning four runs in the last over. Rawtenstall were in the final!

The final was at home against Burnley who posted 253-8. It was always going to be too many for Rawtenstall and they were all out for 173.

The budget to appoint a good professional who could compete in the league was becoming increasingly difficult for some league clubs. Rawtenstall were no exception to this and found difficulty meeting Pelser's demands for **2015** nevertheless he was back for a third year at Bacup Road. It was another good all-round performance from the South African with 702 runs including a century 108 at Colne. Sam Kershaw was again the leading amateur with 545 including his first century for the club, 111 not out, also at Colne. In the above game at Colne they both recorded the highest ever third wicket partnership for the club (202). Chris Cook-Martin hit a valuable 398 in 17 matches and Joe McCluskie, having signed from Bacup, added some strength to the batting and bowing line up with 386 runs and 23 wickets. Keith Roscoe with 67 wickets, including 7-23 at Rishton, was leading bowler with Pelser and Imran Abid each taking 34 scalps.

The team also made the final of the 20/20 competition for the first time, Rawtenstall finished 2nd in their group of seven teams and faced Lowerhouse in the semi-final. Rawtenstall posted 163-4 in their 20 overs with 53 coming from Chris Cook Martin. There was then an inspired bowling display from 23 year old Danny Whittle who took 5-18 off four overs to bowl Lowerhouse out for 127.

The final was against Burnley at Rawtenstall but the Bacup Road men were never in the game after Burnley posted 171 in their 20 overs. Rawtenstall were 105 all out and lost by 66 runs.

In **2016** Rawtenstall made history by signing the Lancashire League's first overseas amateur, Australian Nick Maiolo played in the Western Australia Cricket Association First Grade competition and also had spells playing in Durham. For the last two seasons he had played for Durham City in the Durham League. Maiolo was a top order right handed batsman who bowled left arm spin. The club had been in limbo since their original professional signing Saliya Saman had his application for a visa rejected in May. Maiolo scored 347 runs in his 17 appearances and was supported by Joe McCluskie (343) and Matt Kershaw (327). Roscoe took 37 wickets and McCluskie 25. Wicketkeeper Nick Payne joined an illustrious list in becoming only the third Rawtenstall keeper to take 6 victims in a match. It took place away at Burnley on 17th July. Despite losing the game, Payne took 4 catches and 2 stumpings to join Jack Barnes (1931) and John Jordan (1952) in the record books.

There were many in the town, league and county that wondered if Rawtenstall would be able to fulfil their fixtures for **2017**. Finances and players retiring or moving on would mean early baptisms for many junior players who were clearly not ready. The team would also rely on the goodwill of former players and family friends to turn out on the odd occasion and often would be searching for players at the last minute. Nevertheless the club countered the doom mongers and completed their fixtures although they would finish bottom in both phases of the league.

History was made in the Lancashire League as one new team from the Northern League (Darwen) and two teams from the Ribblesdale League (Clitheroe and Great Harwood) joined. Two of them made an immediate impact with Clitheroe taking the championship and Darwen the runners up spot. It was the first change to the league make-up for over 130 years and whilst some aficionados welcomed the change others felt that it would cause some tensions and issues. There were some murmurings around the outfield and club bars that some teams were paying amateurs in order to compete - indeed many argued and postured that half of some clubs teams were professionals. Of course this is no new phenomenon within the Lancashire League – for years fans have spoken of the "brown envelopes" masonically handed to players behind the sight screens, however it was becoming clear that there were the haves and the have nots in terms of clubs with the resources and cute accounting to pay for more than the stipulated one professional.

The often reliable Roscoe was captain but was struggling himself with a serious illness that required major surgery later in the year. Professional Payne, helping the club out at short notice, hit 510 runs including a century at home to Bacup and after playing for 14 years, Rizwan Shafiq had his best season with the bat scoring 331 runs but that was it. Roscoe was the leading bowler with just 19 wickets.

Captain and wicketkeeper Vinny Hanson (left) called it a day on the playing field and took up duties as club chairman. His figures are very similar to those of Brian Manning (1957 -1986) the main difference being the number of stumpings. A total of 341 catches and 196 stumpings – most of which were collected via the double act of Hanson and Roscoe.

The total of 537 league victims place Hanson at the top of the list as Rawtenstalls leading wicketkeeper. His career record is highlighted below.

Peter Vincent Hanson - Lancashire League Career Batting and Fielding (1996-2017)

M	I	NO	Runs	HS	Ave	100	50	Ct	St
448	359	32	4071	93*	12.44	0	10	341	196

Towards the end of the year the club generated some much needed income by holding its first bonfire and firework display. The Rawtenstall public responded and over 2500 people enjoyed a spectacular firework display. It was the first community event organised by the club for some time and demonstrated that, with a little hard work and organisation, the rewards can be forthcoming. For the club, it generated nearly £10,000, however the real winner was the goodwill and enthusiastic response the club got from the local community. This would give the committee the opportunity and confidence to build upon the positive feedback it had received and encourage them to organise further events.

Keith Roscoe's Lancashire League Bowling Career   * games played for Bacup.

	Balls	Mdns	Runs	Wkts	BB	Ave	4wI	S Rate	Econ	
1979	461	5	309	15	3-33	20.60	0	30.73	4.02	*
1980	640	4	432	25	5-59	17.28	1	25.60	4.05	*
1981	767	6	556	30	8-34	18.53	3	25.56	4.34	*
1982	1318	8	814	49	6-54	16.61	2	26.89	3.70	*
1983	1327	13	914	48	7-62	19.04	4	27.64	4.13	*
1984	1086	5	825	31	6-65	26.61	2	35.03	4.55	*
1985	1436	38	893	44	5-19	20.29	3	32.63	3.73	
1986	1745	46	1105	51	5-36	21.66	2	34.21	3.79	
1987	1415	43	648	49	6-51	13.22	2	28.87	2.74	
1988	1623	30	1046	51	6-37	20.50	4	31.82	3.86	
1989	1679	37	996	45	5-40	22.13	2	37.31	3.55	
1990	1352	26	811	44	7-58	18.43	2	30.72	3.59	
1991	1379	34	904	33	6-71	27.39	1	41.78	3.93	
1992	1704	51	937	54	7-45	17.35	4	31.55	3.29	
1997	1619	54	885	36	6-29	24.58	1	44.97	3.27	
1998	1619	57	899	62	7-45	14.50	5	26.11	3.33	
1999	1910	70	982	56	7-4	17.53	6	34.10	3.08	
2000	2174	72	963	**91**	8-25	10.58	9	23.89	2.65	
2001	1412	51	696	38	7-22	18.31	3	37.15	2.95	
2002	1657	49	913	58	7-101	15.74	6	28.56	3.30	
2003	1617	53	1002	41	**9-77**	24.43	2	39.43	3.71	
2004	1863	71	863	66	7-32	13.07	5	28.22	2.77	
2005	2740	133	1402	84	6-54	16.69	8	32.61	3.07	
2006	1375	47	781	33	5-51	23.66	2	41.66	3.40	
2007	1783	59	919	58	6-48	15.84	5	30.74	3.09	
2008	2062	79	1077	71	7-87	15.16	4	29.04	3.13	
2009	707	27	319	26	6-43	12.26	2	27.19	2.70	
2010	2064	74	1167	73	7-89	15.98	5	28.27	3.39	
2011	2235	65	1390	72	7-33	19.30	7	31.04	3.73	
2012	1687	53	952	53	7-61	17.96	5	31.83	3.38	
2013	1843	55	1080	53	6-35	20.37	2	34.77	3.51	
2014	1964	57	1146	78	6-36	14.69	5	25.17	3.50	
2015	1713	78	811	67	7-23	12.10	5	25.56	2.84	
2016	1446	51	738	37	5-54	19.94	1	39.08	3.06	
2017	1104	30	619	19	3-64	32.57	0	58.10	3.36	

Keith Roscoe

As the **2018** season approached there was news that the club had appointed a certain K Petersen as professional. The whispers in the bars around town were citing an unknown rich benefactor who had come forward with a very large brown envelope. However it wasn't Kevin who the club had signed, but young South African Keegan Peterson - a 24 year old right hand bat, off spin bowler and wicketkeeper.

It would be change again for 2018 in the structure of the competition as the Lancashire League welcomed another seven sides to join (Crompton, Littleborough, Middleton, Milnrow, Norden, Rochdale and Walsden).

The Lancashire League now has 24 teams and everyone associated with it hoped for a season to remember. As it was back in 1886, there will be rivalries, fierce competition, but above all new friendships and associations to be made.

The first week of the season in mid-April was greeted with the news that the League executive had taken the decision to call off all games due to the poor state of the grounds. There had been an unprecedented amount of rainfall for the past few months with many football games also being affected. Rain was no new phenomenon to Lancashire but for a dozen or so years there had been a significant rise in the number of games affected. Two weeks later the May Day holiday weekend saw temperatures soar to their highest on record.

Yes Global Warming had found its way to East Lancashire!

	P	W	T	L	N/R	Bt pts	Bow pts	Total Pts	Position	
2010	**26**	**13**	**1**	**12**	**0**	**13**	**30**	**180**	**7/14**	
2011	26	12		13	1	14	25	162	9/14	
2012	26	4		19	3	6	18	73	14/14	
2013	26	9		12	5	5	25	135	11/14	
2014	26	13		13	0	13	28	171	8/14	
2015	**26**	**12**		**12**	**2**	**9**	**26**	**161**	**7/14**	
2016	26	6		12	8	6	15	105	13/14	
2017	16	1		12	3	0	7	26	17/17	Phase 1
	23	2		15	6	0	10	48	8/8	Phase 2
2018	24									
2019										

Best seasons of the decade in bold

Final Thoughts

As the 125 year anniversary of the Lancashire League begins, all the clubs more than ever before need the support and encouragement from their respective townsfolk to ensure cricket is not only played but thrives for another 100 plus years. For supporters, members and players at Rawtenstall Cricket Club the above reads so true. It's not just cricket clubs that struggle to exist - look at any amateur sports organisation and you will see a few dedicated individuals working over and above what should be expected. Rawtenstall is no exception to this. Too many clubs rely on the goodwill and voluntarism of many folk approaching and some well into and beyond their pension age.

Unfortunately many young men in their 20's and 30's no longer want to dedicate their time to the game as clubs rely upon players into their 40's and 50's. Clubs also continuously look for the support and investment of local people who can give their time and expertise, not just in a playing capacity, but also in the management and organisation, assisting with the maintenance of the ground, organise fundraising events or coaching the junior players.

As the Lancashire League enters a new era with new clubs and new challenges let's hope and wish that the next 100 years offers cricket lovers and the community of Rawtenstall the joy, excitement, competition and camaraderie that the game brings.

Here's to another century at The Worswick Memorial Ground!

Most career runs - League Matches (over 2100 runs)

BOLD = professional   * indicates amateur and professional scores

		M	Inns	NO	Runs	HS	Ave	100	50	
1	PG Wood	513	497	56	14926	148	33.84	12	99	
2	G Barlow	524	507	53	10245	126*	22.56	6	45	
3	**A Payne**	345	312	33	9789	182	35.08	10	64	*
4	J Middleton	447	414	62	7330	166*	20.82	5	25	
5	MC Disley	328	321	40	6666	150*	23.72	4	31	
6	BW Chapman	403	387	37	6415	125	18.32	2	22	
7	F Pickup	265	262	22	6196	130*	25.81	4	39	
8	W Towler	292	291	22	6103	156*	22.68	3	30	
9	RAE Hitch	312	304	24	5929	105	21.17	2	30	
10	B Payne	366	341	43	5515	91	18.50	0	22	
11	T Incles	262	255	29	5508	127*	24.37	1	35	
12	AW Pewtress	250	249	23	5369	122*	23.75	2	28	
13	CJ Cook-Martin	244	223	7	5341	146	24.72	4	30	
14	K Barnes	358	333	53	4852	102*	17.32	1	15	
15	R Waller	431	391	40	4539	86	12.93	0	13	
16	EH Howarth	294	287	40	4153	73	16.81	0	22	
17	BA Manning	518	405	75	4148	81*	12.56	0	6	
18	PV Hanson	448	359	32	4071	93*	12.44	0	10	
19	G Hargreaves	262	258	45	3878	131	18.20	3	11	
20	JM Kershaw	176	174	23	3821	141*	25.30	2	17	
21	K French	251	242	28	3644	102*	17.02	1	18	
22	P White	284	277	20	3526	90	13.71	0	12	
23	N Coupe	449	328	90	3513	99	14.76	0	12	
24	**CG Borde**	127	112	26	3423	111*	39.80	1	28	
25	DG Barlow	267	234	15	3327	81	15.19	0	5	
26	H Clegg	224	221	23	3052	95*	15.41	0	12	
27	RC Howarth	176	172	12	2959	93*	18.49	0	11	
28	RJ Wood	215	200	20	2916	102*	16.20	1	8	
29	H Greenwood	194	182	28	2823	122*	18.33	2	10	
30	PJ Seal	256	202	28	2792	101	16.04	1	10	
31	G Ashworth	383	327	58	2726	60	10.13	0	2	
32	**MP Mott**	50	48	9	2708	161*	69.43	7	19	
33	G Hardy	153	150	15	2698	85*	19.98	0	14	
34	**BJ Pelser**	80	74	12	2630	126	42.41	6	17	
35	G Hoyle	190	171	30	2582	85	18.31	0	8	
36	T Waller	192	176	11	2527	80	15.31	0	12	
37	W Place	142	141	19	2493	111*	20.43	2	11	
38	J Swanney	113	109	19	2475	118*	27.50	1	10	
39	GG Heaton	147	143	19	2387	123	19.25	1	14	
40	JE Downes	205	202	30	2344	63	13.62	0	5	
41	S Wells	364	244	43	2331	86	11.59	0	3	
42	**CR Miller**	78	71	8	2263	115	35.92	3	14	
43	JE Downes	250	245	30	2175	60	10.11	0	3	
44	**VS Hazare**	52	49	16	2116	100*	64.12	2	21	
45	**MG Bevan**	42	41	11	2100	142	70.00	5	14	

League Centurions – Bold = professional * Indicates not out

	Runs	Name	Opponent	Venue	Year
1	182	A Payne	v Colne	Colne	2010
2	173	A Payne	v Nelson	Rawtenstall	2003
3	166*	J Middleton	v Bacup	Rawtenstall	1941
4	**161***	**MP Mott**	v Lowerhouse	Rawtenstall	2001
5	156*	W Towler	v Haslingden	Rawtenstall	1899
6	**155***	**MP Mott**	v Todmorden	Rawtenstall	2000
7	**154***	**LD Ferreira**	v Church	Rawtenstall	1999
8	150*	MC Disley	v East Lancs	Rawtenstall	1908
9	148	PG Wood	v Todmorden	Rawtenstall	1990
10	146	CJ Cook-Martin	v East Lancs	Rawtenstall	2014
11	**142**	**MG Bevan**	v Lowerhouse	Rawtenstall	1993
12	141*	JM Kershaw	v East Lancs	Rawtenstall	1991
13	**137***	**KLT Arthurton**	v Enfield	Enfield	1998
14	**136**	**FD Stephenson**	v East Lancs	Rawtenstall	1982
15	**136**	**MP Mott**	v Burnley	Burnley	2001
16	131	G Hargreaves	v Enfield	Rawtenstall	1941
17	131	PG Wood	v Nelson	Nelson	1991
18	130*	F Pickup	v Nelson	Rawtenstall	1901
19	**129**	**G Leach**	v Ramsbottom	Ramsbottom	1915
20	128*	W Towler	v Rishton	Rawtenstall	1905
21	**128***	**A Payne**	v Bacup	Rawtenstall	2017
22	128	G Fowler	v Todmorden	Rawtenstall	1977
23	127*	T Incles	v Todmorden	Rawtenstall	1957
24	127	PG Wood	v Burnley	Burnley	1988
25	126*	G Barlow	v Church	Rawtenstall	1984
26	126*	PG Wood	v Rishton	Rawtenstall	1994
27	**126**	**BJ Pelser**	v Church	Rawtenstall	2013
28	125	J Middleton	v Bacup	Rawtenstall	1942
29	125	BW Chapman	v Haslingden	Rawtenstall	1973
30	123*	MC Disley	v Todmorden	Todmorden	1903
31	123	GG Heaton	v Church	Rawtenstall	1968
32	123	AJ Clough	v Haslingden	Rawtenstall	2010
33	122*	AW Pewtress	v Rishton	Rawtenstall	1914
34	122*	H Greenwood	v Burnley	Rawtenstall	1941
35	122*	PG Wood	v Accrington	Rawtenstall	1989
36	**122***	**MP Mott**	v Burnley	Burnley	2000
37	**122**	**MJ Smith**	v Rishton	Rishton	2003
38	**120***	**G Leach**	v Bacup	Rawtenstall	1915
39	**120**	**PR Sleep**	v Todmorden	Rawtenstall	1996
40	119*	A Payne	v East Lancs	Rawtenstall	2007
41	**119***	**BJ Pelser**	v Colne	Colne	2013
42	**119**	**KJ Grieves**	v Haslingden	Haslingden	1948
43	**119**	**MG Bevan**	v Accrington	Rawtenstall	1994
44	119	A Payne	v Ramsbottom	Rawtenstall	2003
45	118*	J Swanney	v East Lancs	Rawtenstall	1981
46	118*	**MG Bevan**	v Rishton	Rawtenstall	1994

47	117*	G Barlow	v Lowerhouse	Rawtenstall	1984
48	**116**	**MG Bevan**	v Todmorden	Rawtenstall	1993
49	115*	PG Wood	v Nelson	Rawtenstall	1991
50	**115***	**MP Mott**	v Burnley	Rawtenstall	2001
51	**115***	**AJ Hall**	v Burnley	Rawtenstall	2002
52	**115**	**CR Miller**	v Rishton	Rawtenstall	1990
53	115	AH Taylor	v Burnley	Rawtenstall	1895
54	**114***	**MNR Cooray**	v East Lancs	Rawtenstall	2011
55	113*	MC Disley	v Haslingden	Haslingden	1903
56	113	A Payne	v Bacup	Bacup	2010
57	**112***	**AJ Hall**	v Accrington	Rawtenstall	2002
58	112	RG Watson	v East Lancs	Rawtenstall	1983
59	**112**	**MG Bevan**	v Enfield	Rawtenstall	1993
60	111*	W Place	v Ramsbottom	Rawtenstall	1934
61	**111***	**CG Borde**	v Bacup	Bacup	1961
62	111*	JA Benn	v Ramsbottom	Ramsbottom	1986
63	**111***	**MP Mott**	v Todmorden	Rawtenstall	2001
64	111*	A Payne	v Colne	Colne	2003
65	111*	SJ Kershaw	v Colne	Colne	2015
66	110*	F Pickup	v Haslingden	Haslingden	1901
67	**110***	**H Harrison**	v Haslingden	Haslingden	1911
68	109*	W Place	v Burnley	Rawtenstall	1956
69	**109***	**KLT Arthurton**	v Burnley	Rawtenstall	1998
70	**109***	**BJ Pelser**	v Ramsbottom	Ramsbottom	2013
71	**109**	**BJ Pelser**	v Todmorden	Todmorden	2013
72	108*	G Barlow	v Colne	Rawtenstall	1978
73	108	F Pickup	v Accrington	Accrington	1900
74	**108**	**G Leach**	v Church	Rawtenstall	1914
75	108	PG Wood	v Rishton	Rawtenstall	1980
76	108	CJ Cook-Martin	v Burnley	Burnley	2007
77	**108**	**L Vincent**	v Burnley	Burnley	2011
78	**108**	**BJ Pelser**	v Colne	Colne	2015
79	107*	K Reid	v Enfield	Enfield	1950
80	107*	S Ashworth	v Colne	Rawtenstall	1982
81	107	PG Wood	v Rishton	Rishton	1993
82	107	PG Wood	v Lowerhouse	Rawtenstall	1993
83	**106***	**KLT Arthurton**	v Bacup	Rawtenstall	1998
84	106	W Towler	v Ramsbottom	Ramsbottom	1899
85	**106**	**S Abid Ali**	v Accrington	Rawtenstall	1978
86	106	JM Kershaw	v Colne	Rawtenstall	1991
87	**106**	**MJ Smith**	v Rishton	Rawtenstall	2003
88	105	RAE Hitch	v Accrington	Rawtenstall	1936
89	105	PG Wood	v Ramsbottom	Ramsbottom	1992
90	105	CJ Cook-Martin	v Todmorden	Todmorden	2008
91	104*	F Pickup	v Rishton	Rawtenstall	1899
92	**104***	**CR Miller**	v Church	Rawtenstall	1990
93	**104***	**A Payne**	v Accrington	Accrington	2005
94	104	TG Holt	v Nelson	Rawtenstall	1976
95	104	CJ Cook-Martin	v Lowerhouse	Lowerhouse	2008
96	104	J Rushmore	v Lowerhouse	Rawtenstall	2009

97	103*	H Greenwood	v Accrington	Accrington	1950
98	103*	PG Wood	v Church	Rawtenstall	1978
99	**103***	**CR Miller**	v Accrington	Rawtenstall	1990
100	103*	KLT Arthurton	v Church	Church	1998
101	103*	A Payne	v Ramsbottom	Rawtenstall	2011
102	**103**	**G Leach**	v Church	Church	1913
103	**103**	**S Abid Ali**	v Church	Church	1977
104	**103**	**MP Mott**	v Ramsbottom	Rawtenstall	2000
105	102*	G Hargreaves	v Church	Rawtenstall	1937
106	102*	GH Bradshaw	v Accrington	Rawtenstall	1954
107	102*	K Barnes	v Lowerhouse	Rawtenstall	1959
108	102*	BW Chapman	v Lowerhouse	Rawtenstall	1970
109	102*	K French	v Lowerhouse	Rawtenstall	1974
110	102*	RJ Wood	v Rishton	Rawtenstall	2002
111	102	MC Disley	v Haslingden	Haslingden	1910
112	102	J Middleton	v Enfield	Rawtenstall	1931
113	102	A Payne	v Burnley	Rawtenstall	2002
114	101*	J Middleton	v Enfield	Rawtenstall	1932
115	101*	J Middleton	v Haslingden	Rawtenstall	1937
116	101*	G Hargreaves	v Rishton	Rishton	1938
117	101	AW Pewtress	v East Lancs	Rawtenstall	1914
118	101*	G Barlow	v Enfield	Rawtenstall	1979
119	101*	G Barlow	v Bacup	Bacup	1983
120	101*	G Barlow	v Accrington	Rawtenstall	1997
121	**101***	**BJ Pelser**	v Nelson	Rawtenstall	2014
122	101	RAE Hitch	v Accrington	Accrington	1933
123	101	PJ Seal	v Colne	Rawtenstall	2004
124	**100***	**VS Hazare**	v Todmorden	Rawtenstall	1955
125	**100***	**VS Hazare**	v Enfield	Enfield	1955
126	**100***	**LA King**	v Nelson	Rawtenstall	1965
127	100	PG Wood	v Church	Rawtenstall	1977
128	**100***	**KLT Arthurton**	v Church	Rawtenstall	1998
129	**100**	**KLT Arthurton**	v Enfield	Rawtenstall	1998
130	100	J Kerrigan	v Accrington	Rawtenstall	2011

Venues
Rawtenstall 89.
Burnley 5, Colne 5, Haslingden 5, Ramsbottom 5, Accrington 4, Bacup 3, Church 3, Enfield 3, Rishton 3, Todmorden 3, Nelson 1, Lowerhouse 1, East Lancashire 0.

Opposition
Accrington 13, Church 13, Burnley 12, Rishton 12, Todmorden 11, Colne 9, East Lancashire 9, Enfield 9, Haslingden 9, Lowerhouse 9, Ramsbottom 9, Bacup 8, Nelson 7.

Highest Partnerships in League Games

Runs	First Wicket	Opposition	Venue	Year
193*	G Barlow 126* & PS Pickles 65*	Church	Rawtenstall	1984
191	G Leach 129 & T Waller 72	Ramsbottom	Ramsbottom	1915
190	JM Kershaw 81 & PG Wood 107	Rishton	Rishton	1993
	Second Wicket			
239*	PG Wood 126* & MG Bevan 118*	Rishton	Rawtenstall	1994
227	PG Wood 107 & MG Bevan 142	Lowerhouse	Rawtenstall	1993
209	AJ Clough 92 & L Vincent 08	Burnley	Burnley	2011
	Third Wicket			
202	SJ Kershaw 111* & BJ Pelser 108	Colne	Colne	2015
182	W Towler 156* & G Hardy 69*	Haslingden	Rawtenstall	1899
	Fourth Wicket			
200*	MNR Cooray 90* & A Payne 103*	Ramsbottom	Rawtenstall	2011
193*	MNR Cooray 114* & A Payne 73*	East Lancs	Rawtenstall	2011
162	A Payne 90 & RJ Wood 79	East Lancs	Rawtenstall	2003
	Fifth Wicket			
151	H Greenwood 103* & RH Whittaker 53	Accrington	Accrington	1950
141*	BJ Pelser 57* & PSR Wrathmell 69*	Colne	Rawtenstall	2013
127	BJ Pelser 83 & D Guest 46	Church	Rawtenstall	2011
	Sixth Wicket			
114*	E Poole 64* & G Hoyle 51*	Enfield	Rawtenstall	1937
108*	W Towler 60* & H Harrison 51*	Haslingden	Rawtenstall	1911
102*	BJ Pelser 62* & GR Bevan 50*	Bacup	Bacup	2014
	Seventh Wicket			
119	G Barlow 101* & P Rush 48	Accrington	Rawtenstall	1997
111	DG Barlow 47 & PV Hanson 93*	Church	Rawtenstall	2003
	Eighth Wicket			
101	MP Mott 115* & AJ Clough 26	Burnley	Rawtenstall	2001
83	WB Haughton 52* & FW Nicholls 30*	Bacup	Bacup	1953
	Ninth Wicket			
74	G Holt 53 & WB Haughton 22*	Todmorden	Rawtenstall	1954
	Tenth Wicket			
76*	PA Riding 41* & J Beaumont 37*	Accrington	Accrington	1982
68	R Haworth 24* & J Griffiths 41	East Lancs	East Lancs	1921
66	RH Madden 71 & H Wells 26*	Nelson	Nelson	1952

Highest individual Innings in a Worsley Cup game (80+)

Bold denotes professional, (*not out)

	Name	Opponent	Venue	Year
147	A Payne	Colne	Colne	2003
144	**MG Bevan**	**Enfield**	**Rawtenstall**	**1993**
132	CJ Cook-Martin	Todmorden	Rawtenstall	2008
129	**MJ Smith**	**Nelson**	**Rawtenstall**	**2003**
125	PV Hanson	Rishton	Rawtenstall	2014
124	**MG Bevan**	**Church**	**Rawtenstall**	**1993**
119*	**S Abid Ali**	**East Lancashire**	**Rawtenstall**	**1978**
118	**KM Curran**	**Haslingden**	**Haslingden**	**1983**
118*	**MP Mott**	**Todmorden**	**Todmorden**	**2000**
113	A Payne	East Lancashire	Rawtenstall	2006
109*	G Croisdale	Lowerhouse	Rawtenstall	1975
106	J Middleton	Bacup	Bacup	1929
99	JM Kershaw	Church	Rawtenstall	1990
97	T Waller	Bacup	Bacup	1927
93	G Barlow	Haslingden	Haslingden	1986
92	**VS Hazare**	**Haslingden**	**Rawtenstall**	**1955**
92	**VE Jackson**	**Bacup**	**Rawtenstall**	**1958**
91	JW Grant	East Lancashire	Rawtenstall	1968
91	**MG Bevan**	**Bacup**	**Rawtenstall**	**1993**
91	SJ Kershaw	Nelson	Nelson	2013
89	P White	Haslingden	Rawtenstall	1955
87	G Barlow	Todmorden	Rawtenstall	1978
87*	**BJ Pelser**	**Burnley**	**Rawtenstall**	**2014**
86	B Payne	Haslingden	Haslingden	1983
86*	R Swift	Burnley	Rawtenstall	1988
86	**BJ Pelser**	**Ramsbottom**	**Ramsbottom**	**2014**
85	**A Payne**	**East Lancashire**	**East Lancs**	**2004**
84	RC Howarth	Bacup	Bacup	1935
84	**VS Hazare**	**Rishton**	**Rawtenstall**	**1955**
83	PG Wood	East Lancashire	Rawtenstall	1978
82*	B Payne	Colne	Colne	1978
81	**CR Miller**	**Burnley**	**Rawtenstall**	**1992**
80	CJ Cook-Martin	Lowerhouse	Rawtenstall	2014

Venues: Rawtenstall 21, Bacup 3, Haslingden 3, Colne 2, East Lancs 1, Nelson 1, Ramsbottom 1, Todmorden 1.

Opposition: Bacup 5, East Lancs 5, Haslingden 5, Burnley 3, Todmorden 3, Church 2, Colne 2, Lowerhouse 2, Nelson 2, Rishton 2, Enfield 1, Ramsbottom 1, Accrington 0.

Leading wicket takers League Games (Bold denotes professional)

* Includes both amateur and professional figures

		Balls	Mdns	Runs	Wkts	Best	Ave	5 Wkts
1	K Roscoe	48927	1590	26944	1543	9-77	17.46	108
2	**RG Hardstaff**	**15755**	**884**	**6731**	**702**	**9-23**	**9.75**	**72**
3	R Banks	24147	425	10278	634	8-16	16.21	38
4	N Coupe	21584	510	9237	533	8-35	17.33	21
5	S Wells	19828	298	8913	521	7-11	17.10	25
6	R Waller	14887	351	8095	473	7-17	17.11	28
7	J Middleton	14760	265	7492	439	7-49	17.06	16
8	**E Smith**	**10997**	**483**	**3891**	**420**	**9-19**	**9.26**	**46**
9	G Ashworth	13724	438	6180	413	7-22	14.96	19
10	G Croisdale	16160	284	8148	402	7-16	20.26	18
*11	A Payne	13619	437	7250	386	8-51	18.78	18
12	**JW Grant**	**7903**	**218**	**2973**	**309**	**9-29**	**9.62**	**35**
13	**G Ramsbottom**	**8492**	**345**	**3328**	**304**	**9-15**	**11.31**	**24**
14	**CG Borde**	**8631**	**120**	**4212**	**304**	**8-40**	**13.85**	**25**
15	B Storey	13902	298	8012	300	6-36	26.70	2
16	**TJ Nicholson**	**7374**	**466**	**3085**	**299**	**8-22**	**10.67**	**27**
17	PJ Seal	11414	313	7154	296	7-55	24.16	9
18	T Waller	8807	285	3838	290	7-10	13.23	19
19	**CR Miller**	**8313**	**262**	**4451**	**283**	**9-31**	**15.72**	**23**
20	Rod Taylor	11226	170	6024	282	6-18	21.36	10
21	**SF Barnes**	**6231**	**310**	**2274**	**278**	**9-20**	**8.17**	**31**
22	**AG Slater**	**8288**	**355**	**3305**	**267**	**9-45**	**12.37**	**23**
23	**G Leach**	**6279**	**171**	**3096**	**264**	**9-32**	**11.72**	**28**
24	R Holmes	8424	203	5074	244	8-17	20.79	8
25	**S Abid Ali**	**8869**	**208**	**3548**	**236**	**7-44**	**15.03**	**14**
26	MC Disley	7685	191	4257	235	8-36	18.58	9
27	F Haworth	6026	127	3365	226	9-21	14.88	15
28	**T Stringer**	**4231**	**128**	**2070**	**214**	**9-32**	**9.67**	**24**
29	**GE Tribe**	**4943**	**75**	**2070**	**212**	**8-27**	**9.76**	**26**
30	**FD Stephenson**	**5462**	**115**	**2464**	**211**	**9-60**	**11.67**	**21**
31	RM Shafiq	8619	206	5981	206	6-38	29.03	5
32	**TW Foster**	**4778**	**236**	**2284**	**191**	**9-22**	**12.21**	**14**
33	**J Cook**	**5428**	**334**	**1776**	**191**	**8-28**	**9.29**	**17**
34	H Hannah	6455	129	2990	187	7-15	15.98	10
35	F Hamer	5466	190	2757	180	6-38	15.31	9
36	**KJ Grieves**	**5122**	**109**	**1968**	**173**	**7-15**	**11.37**	**15**
37	**VS Hazare**	**5406**	**127**	**2011**	**160**	**7-14**	**12.56**	**13**
38	**TA Merrick**	**4836**	**143**	**2469**	**158**	**7-37**	**15.62**	**12**
39	**RD Burrows**	**4260**	**151**	**1860**	**153**	**9-11**	**12.15**	**16**
40	P Rush	7060	121	4964	152	6-47	32.65	3
41	J Kelly	4656	103	2562	151	7-34	17.19	10
42	**H Harrison**	**4344**	**130**	**1872**	**149**	**8-20**	**12.56**	**16**
43	J Beaumont	5609	96	3126	139	7-14	22.48	6
44	**BJ Pelser**	**5002**	**140**	**2593**	**129**	**6-42**	**20.10**	**4**
45	**LA King**	**4910**	**104**	**1996**	**128**	**7-23**	**15.59**	**9**
46	Imran Abid	4033	93	2612	127	6-51	20.56	6
47	R Glover	5870	137	4128	125	5-34	33.02	4
48	Ross Taylor	4755	104	1956	122	7-25	16.03	4
49	**VE Jackson**	**4464**	**114**	**1790**	**122**	**6-29**	**14.67**	**10**
50	W Towler	3656	102	2190	118	6-36	18.55	6

Best bowling in an Innings in Lancashire League matches – 8 wickets or more.
Bold denotes amateur

		Name	Opposition	Venue	Year
1	9-11	RD Burrows	Bacup	Bacup	1920
2	9-15	G Ramsbottom	Lowerhouse	Lowerhouse	1901
3	9-19	E Smith	Lowerhouse	Rawtenstall	1925
4	9-20	SF Barnes	Burnley	Rawtenstall	1932
5	**9-21**	**F Haworth**	**Burnley**	**Rawtenstall**	**1916**
6	9-22	TW Foster	Lowerhouse	Lowerhouse	1898
7	9-23	RG Hardstaff	Bacup	Bacup	1893
8	9-29	JW Grant	Accrington	Rawtenstall	1968
9	9-31	CR Miller	Burnley	Rawtenstall	1991
10	9-32	T Stringer	Todmorden	Todmorden	1904
11	9-32	G Leach	Enfield	Enfield	1913
12	9-33	RG Hardstaff	Colne	Rawtenstall	1895
13	9-36	JW Grant	Church	Rawtenstall	1970
14	9-42	AK Walker	Enfield	Enfield	1954
15	9-43	E Smith	Ramsbottom	Rawtenstall	1925
16	9-45	E Smith	Todmorden	Todmorden	1925
17	9-45	AG Slater	Church	Rawtenstall	1936
18	9-55	T Stringer	Nelson	Rawtenstall	1904
19	9-55	G Leach	East Lancs	Blackburn	1915
20	9-55	SF Barnes	Ramsbottom	Ramsbottom	1933
21	9-60	FD Stephenson	Colne	Colne	1982
22	**9-77**	**K Roscoe**	**Colne**	**Colne**	**2003**
23	8-?	TJ Nicholson	Nelson	Rawtenstall	1894
24	8-16	T Stringer	Accrington	Accrington	1905
25	8-16	G Ramsbottom	Lowerhouse	Lowerhouse	1909
26	**8-16**	**R Banks**	**Todmorden**	**Todmorden**	**1940**
27	8-16	AK Walker	East Lancs	Rawtenstall	1954
28	**8-17**	**R Holmes**	**Accrington**	**Accrington**	**1993**
29	8-18	TW Foster	East Lancs	Blackburn	1898
30	8-18	E Smith	Burnley	Burnley	1926
31	8-20	RG Hardstaff	Ramsbottom	Ramsbottom	1896
32	8-20	H Harrison	Rishton	Rawtenstall	1912
33	8-21	AG Slater	Bacup	Rawtenstall	1935
34	8-22	TJ Nicholson	Bury	Rawtenstall	1893
35	8-22	AG Slater	Ramsbottom	Rawtenstall	1936
36	8-23	FD Stephenson	Accrington	Accrington	1981
37	8-24	SF Barnes	Ramsbottom	Rawtenstall	1931
38	8-24	FD Stephenson	Todmorden	Rawtenstall	1981
39	**8-25**	**K Roscoe**	**Rishton**	**Rawtenstall**	**2000**
40	8-27	GE Tribe	Church	Rawtenstall	1951
41	8-27	ISL Hewett	Ramsbottom	Rawtenstall	1997
42	8-28	H Harrison	Lowerhouse	Rawtenstall	1912
43	8-28	J Cook	Ramsbottom	Ramsbottom	1922
44	8-28	E Smith	East Lancs	Rawtenstall	1926
45	8-28	SF Barnes	Lowerhouse	Rawtenstall	1932

46	8-29	JW Sunderland	Haslingden	Rawtenstall	1929
47	8-29	JW Grant	Nelson	Rawtenstall	1968
48	8-29	A Worsick	Ramsbottom	Rawtenstall	1979
49	8-29	CR Miller	Lowerhouse	Lowerhouse	1991
50	8-30	T Stringer	Enfield	Enfield	1904
51	8-30	J Cook	Todmorden	Todmorden	1922
52	8-30	GJ Whittall	East Lancs	Blackburn	1996
53	8-31	JW Grant	Ramsbottom	Rawtenstall	1967
54	8-32	T Stringer	Church	Church	1904
55	**8-32**	**P White**	**Haslingden**	**Haslingden**	**1953**
56	8-33	RD Burrows	Church	Rawtenstall	1920
57	8-33	SF Barnes	East Lancs	Rawtenstall	1931
58	8-34	E Smith	Accrington	Rawtenstall	1925
59	8-35	RG Hardstaff	Enfield	Rawtenstall	1898
60	8-35	VJ Evans	Colne	Colne	1939
61	**8-35**	**N Coupe**	**Ramsbottom**	**Rawtenstall**	**1943**
62	8-35	Naved Arif	Lowerhouse	Rawtenstall	2010
63	**8-36**	**MC Disley**	**Lowerhouse**	**Lowerhouse**	**1902**
64	8-36	CR Miller	Nelson	Rawtenstall	1990
65	8-37	E Smith	Colne	Colne	1926
66	8-38	P Sharples	East Lancs	Blackburn	1930
67	8-40	T Stringer	Bacup	Rawtenstall	1904
68	**8-40**	**J Stansfield**	**Church**	**Rawtenstall**	**1916**
69	8-40	GE Tribe	Accrington	Accrington	1950
70	8-40	CG Borde	Colne	Colne	1962
71	8-43	E Smith	Enfield	Enfield	1928
72	8-43	SF Barnes	Lowerhouse	Lowerhouse	1932
73	8-44	T Stringer	Lowerhouse	Rawtenstall	1904
74	8-45	GE Tribe	Ramsbottom	Rawtenstall	1951
75	8-46	RG Hardstaff	Ramsbottom	Ramsbottom	1899
76	8-46	LW Cook	Enfield	Rawtenstall	1924
77	8-47	G Ramsbottom	Haslingden	Haslingden	1908
78	8-47	E Smith	Colne	Colne	1925
79	**8-49**	**F Haworth**	**Nelson**	**Rawtenstall**	**1916**
80	8-51	G Leach	Bacup	Rawtenstall	1913
81	8-51	A Payne	Bacup	Rawtenstall	2005
82	8-52	E Smith	Ramsbottom	Ramsbottom	1928
83	8-56	GE Tribe	Church	Rawtenstall	1950
84	8-57	SF Barnes	Enfield	Rawtenstall	1931
85	8-57	JW Grant	Rishton	Rawtenstall	1968
86	8-57	GT Ross	Ramsbottom	Rawtenstall	1980
87	8-59	H Harrison	Enfield	Enfield	1912
88	8-67	FD Stephenson	Church	Rawtenstall	1982
89	8-70	E Smith	Burnley	Burnley	1925
90	8-94	E Smith	Enfield	Rawtenstall	1928

<u>Venues:</u> Rawtenstall 49, Colne 6, Lowerhouse 6, Enfield 5, Ramsbottom 5, Accrington 4, East Lancs 4, Todmorden 4, Bacup 2, Burnley 2, Haslingden 2, Church 1, Nelson 0, Rishton 0.

<u>Opposition:</u> Ramsbottom 14, Lowerhouse 11, Enfield 9, Church 8, Colne 7, East Lancs 7, Accrington 6, Bacup 6, Burnley 5, Nelson 5, Todmorden 5, Haslingden 3, Rishton 3, Bury 1.

Best bowling in an innings Worsley Cup (top 30) bold denotes amateur

	Name	Opponent	Venue	Year
9-21	**R Banks**	**Ramsbottom**	**Rawtenstall**	**1960**
9-25	CR Miller	Bacup	Bacup	1990
8-34	E Smith	Accrington	Rawtenstall	1925
7-33	TA Merrick	Church	Church	1986
7-35	S Abid Ali	Burnley	Rawtenstall	1976
7-40	**C Flood**	**Accrington**	**Rawtenstall**	**1976**
7-45	CG Borde	Bacup	Rawtenstall	1960
7-50	VE Jackson	Church	Rawtenstall	1957
7-54	CR Miller	Todmorden	Rawtenstall	1990
7-61	TA Merrick	East Lancashire	Blackburn	1985
7-63	DA Renneberg	Church	Church	1969
7-74	GE Tribe	Bacup	Bacup	1950
6-27	**R Banks**	**Bacup**	**Rawtenstall**	**1948**
6-27	VS Hazare	Haslingden	Rawtenstall	1949
6-30	**R Banks**	**Colne**	**Rawtenstall**	**1957**
6-31	AK Walker	Haslingden	Haslingden	1953
6-31	**J Guy**	**Ramsbottom**	**Ramsbottom**	**1961**
6-32	A Worsick	Haslingden	Haslingden	1979
6-36	P Sharples	Haslingden	Haslingden	1930
6-36	**K Roscoe**	**Burnley**	**Burnley**	**1997**
6-37	TA Merrick	Haslingden	Haslingden	1986
6-47	VS Hazare	Ramsbottom	Rawtenstall	1955
6-51	JW Holder	Nelson	Nelson	1974
6-51	**K Roscoe**	**East Lancashire**	**Blackburn**	**1992**
6-54	**R Taylor**	**Nelson**	**Nelson**	**1967**
6-57	S Abid Ali	Enfield	Rawtenstall	1977
6-65	KM Curran	Haslingden	Haslingden	1983
6-66	**K Roscoe**	**Nelson**	**Nelson**	**1987**
6-74	SF Barnes	Bacup	Rawtenstall	1931
6-78	GE Tribe	Ramsbottom	Rawtenstall	1950

Venues: Rawtenstall 14, Haslingden 5, Nelson 3, Bacup 2, Church 2, East Lancs 2, Ramsbottom 1, Burnley 1.

Opposition: Haslingden 6, Bacup 5, Ramsbottom 4, Church 3, Nelson 3, Accrington 2, Burnley 2, East Lancs 2, Colne 1, Enfield 1, Todmorden 1, Lowerhouse 0, Rishton 0.

Wicket Keeping Records - Most victims in a league game

Total	Ct	St	Name	Opponent	Ground	Year
6	1	5	JW Barnes	Enfield	Enfield	1931
6	2	4	J Jordan	East Lancashire	East Lancs	1952
6	4	2	NJ Payne	Burnley	Burnley	2016
5	4	1	JW Barnes	Bacup	Bacup	1934
5	2	3	JW Barnes	East Lancashire	East Lancs	1940
5	4	1	BW Chapman	Ramsbottom	Rawtenstall	1960
5	2	3	P Barnes	Burnley	Rawtenstall	1987
5	4	1	P Barnes	Burnley	Burnley	1994
5	3	2	PV Hanson	Enfield	Enfield	2000
5	2	3	PV Hanson	Church	Church	2001
5	3	2	PV Hanson	Lowerhouse	Lowerhouse	2004
5	4	1	GR Bevan	Great Harwood	Rawtenstall	2017

Most victims in a Worsley Cup game

Total	Ct	St	Name	Opponent	Ground	Year
5	4	1	JW Barnes	Rishton	Rawtenstall	1937
4	3	1	BA Manning	Colne	Rawtenstall	1985
4	2	2	P Barnes	Church	Rawtenstall	1990
4	4	0	J Hallows	Lowerhouse	Lowerhouse	2017
3	3	0	GB Fenton	East Lancs	Rawtenstall	1922
3	1	2	JW Haworth	Todmorden	Rawtenstall	1923
3	3	0	N Coupe	Bacup	Rawtenstall	1937
3	3	0	P Colbourne	Ramsbottom	Rawtenstall	1955
3	1	2	BA Manning	Church	Church	1986
3	3	0	P Barnes	Accrington	Rawtenstall	1993
3	2	1	PV Hanson	Burnley	Burnley	1997
3	2	1	PV Hanson	Ramsbottom	Ramsbottom	2001

Highest number of victims (more than 30)

Victims	Ct	St	Name	Year
46	22	24	PV Hanson	2000
40	30	10	P Barnes	1990
40	25	15	PV Hanson	2014
39	19	20	J Jordan	1951
38	27	11	P Barnes	1994
37	18	19	P Barnes	1987
36	28	8	P Barnes	1988
35	24	11	PV Hanson	2004
35	16	19	PV Hanson	2010
33	14	19	JW Barnes	1932
33	21	12	BA Manning	1971
33	22	11	P Barnes	1992
33	25	8	P Barnes	1993
33	19	14	PV Hanson	2005
32	16	16	JW Barnes	1934
31	29	2	P Barnes	1995
31	25	6	PV Hanson	2001
31	16	15	PV Hanson	2008

Rawtenstall positions in the Lancashire league 1891- 2016

Position	Years	Total
1st	1894,1904,1906,1926,1976,1981,1982,	7
2nd	1936,1940,1947,1949,1950,1967,1968,1987,2007,2008	10
3rd	1896,1897,1898,1937,1951,1970,1972,1980,1990,1993,	10
4th	1893,1902,1914,1952,1979,1988,1989,2004,	8
5th	1895,1900,1931,1945,1948,1958,1961,2001,	8
6th	1919,1924,1932,1934,1984,1985,	6
7th	1892,1899,1907,1918,1923,1927,1942,1946,1975,1978 1991,2002,2005,2010,2015,	15
8th	1901,1911,1935,1943,1959,1960,1962,1971,1992,2014,	10
9th	1912,1921,1939,1957,1965,1974,1977,2011,	8
10th	1906,1910,1913,1938,1941,1955,	6
11th	1905,1908,1915,1928,1929,1953,1954,1964 1983,1994,2000,2013,	12
12th	1891,1916,1925,1956,1966,1998,2003,2006,	8
13th	1909,1963,1969,1973,1986,1995,1996,2016,	8
14th	1903,1920,1930,1933,1944,1997,1999,2009,2012,	9

#0128 - 010618 - C0 - 229/152/9 - CC - DID2211143